Principles of Operating Systems

By Darrell Hajek and Cesar Herrera

Darrell Hajek received his PhD. In mathematics in 1971 from the University of Florida. He was immediately hired by the University of Puerto Rico at Mayaguez (RUM) and has been working there ever since, teaching mathematics and computer science.

In addition to a number of research publications, Dr. Hajek has previously written one computer related book: Assembler Language Programming on the 80x86 Processor (no longer available) which was used as a text at RUM for several years. More recently, he has written a computer graphics text "Introduction to Computer Graphics" (which has also come out in a 2018 edition) and a book of fiction/fantasy: "The Life and Times of Harry Wolf" (with further editions, "Expanded Edition", "Augmented Expanded Edition" and "2018 Edition"

Cesar Herrera worked in industry for several years. He received his MS in computer science from Ohio State University in 1985., and was hired by the University of Puerto Rico at Mayaguez (RUM). . He served as an advisor in the development of the undergraduate computer science program in the Department of Mathematical Sciences, and as coordinator of the undergraduate computer science program for several years. Recently retired, he was a full professor at RUM. He has several publications in software engineering and human-computer interaction and was the primary teacher of operating systems in the Department of Mathematical Sciences for approximately 15 years. He is currently working as a consultant to academic institutions, providing expertise in the areas of databases and human computer interaction

Other books by Hajek and Herrera

Introduction to Computers

Introduction to Computers 2018 Edition

Other books by Darrell Hajek

Introduction to Computer Graphics

Introduction to Computer Graphics 2018 Edition

Life and Times of Harry Wolf

Life and Times of Harry Wolf Expanded Edition

Life and Times of Harry Wolf Augmented Expanded Edition

Life and Times of Harry Wolf 2018 Edition

Preface:

We have noticed that very few students in our operating systems course were purchasing the assigned text. We quickly learned that they found it too expensive. Several (it is rumored) had resorted to downloading (illegal) electronic versions.

Not wanting to motivate illegal activities on the part of our students, we have set out to produce a more reasonably priced alternative.

We have tried to include all the material necessary for a basic course in operating systems, but, in order to keep a low price for our students, we have attempted to keep the content to ONLY what would be necessary for such a course. We fully expect that many will disagree with the choices we have made, both in what we have included and (probably even more) in what we have failed to include. We will revisit these decisions when we prepare future editions. Suggestions and recommendations are welcome.

We will be creating a set of supplementary PowerPoint files for the text as well as a testbank. We will be happy to make both available to any teacher who chooses to adopt the book as assigned text for a course.

You are welcome to contact us at either

darrell.hajek@upr.edu

or cesar.herrera@upr.edu .

Contents

1. Introduction

A computer system consists of several hardware components

processor, memory, system busses, storage devices (hard disk, optical drive, …), input devices (keyboard, mouse, …), output devices (monitor, printer, …)

as well as a LOT of software,

all of which can be considered as being in one of two classes: operating system software and application software.

The operating system is an important part of the software of any computer system. An operating system has several functions. These functions include:

controlling access to the processor(s)

providing a set of services to users of the system (determining how they can interact with the system)

managing system hardware components.

1.0 Computing Systems

The primary function of a computing system is to process data.

The hardware components of a computing system that are managed by the operating system will generally include:

One or more **processing unit(s)**

A processing unit (also referred to as a CPU) controls the operation of the computer and performs the data processing functions. It executes the commands that result in the processing of the system's data.

Memory

Computer memory is often referred to using various names: main memory, primary storage, memory, primary memory, random access memory, RAM.

RAM is "volatile", which means it loses its contents when the computer is shut down

Both the data being processed, as well as the codes for the commands that control the actions of the CPU are stored in RAM.

Input device(s)

Devices that allow the user(s) to enter data into the system's memory as well as to indicate activities that the user might want performed.

Common input devices are keyboards and pointing devices such as trackballs or mice.

Output device(s)

Devices that communicate information *to* users. Devices such as monitors and printers.

External storage devices

Devices where data and information are stored for future use/reference. Hard drives, optical (CD, DVD) drives

Communications device(s)

Devices that transfer data to and from other computing systems. Modems, routers.

System Buses

Electrical connectors which allow the system to move information/data from one device to another.

The operating system involves several functions;

It uses the system's resources, and controls access to them.

It provides a set of services for system users and manages secondary memory and I/O devices.

It controls the operation of the computer, and performs necessary data processing functions,

Its *I/O modules* provide control of movement of data between the computer and external environments, including: storage devices, communications equipment and other I/O devices.

1.0.1 How the Computing System Functions (Simplified)

The system memory (RAM) is divided into a number of cells, each of which has a numerical *address*. In some of the cells there will be codes for instructions that, when executed by the CPU, will cause the computer to process some data in the way that a user wants it processed.

The CPU has a register called the program counter, or PC. The PC will normally contain the address of one of the cells in memory.

The computer system functions by continually repeating three steps as follows:

1. The contents of the cell whose address is in the PC are transferred (copied) into the CPU (data transfer by means of one of the system buses)

2. The contents of the PC register are incremented so that it no longer has the address of the same memory cell and the uploaded data is interpreted as the code for a CPU instruction.
3. The CPU executes that instruction.

1.1   Operating Systems

Most readers will be at least somewhat familiar with the term "operating system". They will have made use of more than one and, if pressed, could probably name some operating systems (UNIX, Linux, Windows, Android, IOS ...) Many, however, would have difficulty in describing just what an operating system IS.

An Operating System is a program, or collection of programs, that manages the resources of a computer system, and provides interfaces between users, system hardware, software, and peripherals.

Operating Systems are among the most complex pieces of software ever developed

An operating system would include (sub) programs that provide interfaces for:

*   users with hardware;
*   users with software;
*   software with hardware;
*   software with other software.

Among the services offered by an operating system will be:

Aids in program development (editors, debuggers)

Program execution (loading program into memory and initiating execution)

Access to I/O devices (hidden procedure to users),

Controlled access to files (information protection),

System access (resource protection- user identification and authorization),

Error detection and response (division by zero, attempt to access forbidden memory location),

Accounting (statistics for various resources).

An operating system will perform tasks like transferring data between main memory and secondary storage and like rendering output onto a display device.

In our modern world, new kinds of hardware and software are continually being created, and any computing system is likely to incorporate some of these at various times in its lifetime. The operating system, then, must be capable of evolving over time in order to deal with changing system environments.

1.2 A Short History of Operating System Development

1.2.1 The earliest computers

(These were not really what we would call computers, today. By modern standards, they were little more than huge calculating devices.) They were "programmed" by setting combinations of switches and connecting wires between appropriate locations on circuit boards. When everything was set up correctly (at least they *hoped* it was set up correctly) the main switch would be thrown and the "program" would start to execute. Output was often communicated by means of display lights on a console. There was nothing even remotely resembling what we would call an operating system. It would require a great deal of time just to set up a program to run. Users would access the computer one after another (in "series" so to speak.) Most installations used a simple sign-up sheet to reserve computer time, and of course, there were scheduling problems. Some of the programs would turn out to require more time than their allocation, and this would result in hard feelings (at best.) Many programs would require less time than reserved, and this would result in wasted computer time, when the system was sitting idle waiting for the next user, who could not be counted on to come before his scheduled time.

The system described above was extremely slow (and error prone.) Computing systems were extremely expensive, and people who have invested lots of money to purchase a computer system generally like to get as much computing out of it as possible. Efficiency and speed were the primary motivating factors in most of the early computer development.

1.2.2 Von Neumann Architecture and serial batch processing systems

Probably the first really major step forward came when Von Neumann proposed a system in which a computer program (as a sequence of binary codes for computer actions) might be stored in, and executed from, computer memory. Programs (and their data) could be read into computer memory (usually from punched cards or paper tape) before being executed. This motivated the first primitive operating systems, which were developed in the mid-1950s. These were small *supervisor programs* (resident monitors) that provided basic I/O operations (such as control of punch card and/or tape readers and printers.) Not only can a machine read a deck of punched card a lot faster than a technician can figure out which sequence of switches to throw, but these systems allowed the system operators to submit sequences ("batches") of programs, to be read one after another. These systems were described as "batch processing systems." The system could read a program, execute it and immediately begin reading the next, without having to wait for the operator to load it.

It was almost immediately recognized that user programs should not be allowed to read or write from the section of memory occupied and used by the resident monitor. Systems were designed to operate in different execution modes:

user mode (in which the programs were restricted to memory access with specific addresses and were not allowed to execute certain commands)

kernel mode (for the operating system only, in which the program would be less restricted as to its memory references and would be allowed to execute a wider range of commands.)

The inclusion of an operating system clearly adds overhead to the system. Operating systems are programs that occupy space in memory and they take time to execute, but are not, themselves, application programs. They are not programs submitted by users for execution. Nevertheless, even the simplest serial batch processing systems produced major improvements in efficiency and throughput of computing systems[1]. Loading a new pack of cards or mounting a new roll of tape requires a very long time (as computers experience time) but it does not take an operator much longer to load cards (or tape) for a sequence of four or five programs than it does to load just one.

1.2.3   Several Programs in Memory at the Same Time

Then somebody figured out that very few programs actually use all the computer memory available, and that, as a consequence, it would usually be possible to fit the code (and data) for more than one program into memory at the same time. If they did that, when one program finished, the system could go directly to executing the next one. With the next program already in memory there would be no loss of time. The system would not have to wait for the cards or tape to start being read. Meanwhile, the operators could be loading the next set of cards or roll of tape while the original sequence of programs was running.

Obviously, these systems required rather more sophisticated "supervisor programs" since they had more things to supervise. It was necessary to keep track of where each program was located in memory, not only to know where to start the next program, but also in order to prevent an executing program from overwriting another waiting program (or the operating system itself.). In addition, the system would have to recognize when a program had finished, and, if there

---

[1]   For one thing, the work of setting up the program was all done offline and did not take up time that the computer might be running.

were more than one waiting program, it would have to select which would be executed next.

1.2.4 Multiprogramming

These early systems typically loaded all their data together with the programs, but, as computers began to be used for larger and larger collections of data, the amount of computer memory available in a system began to put uncomfortable constraints on the amount of data that could be processed, and designers turned to external data storage (primarily tape) in order to deal with larger data sets. Of course, this meant that even more complex operating systems were required, systems that could provide interfaces with these new kinds of external devices. It also meant that programmers were beginning to write programs that would attempt to access data stored on one of these external devices. When one of these programs would do that (and it was starting to happen more and more frequently) the program would have to stop executing and wait for the data to be copied into memory where the program could make use of it. It was also becoming common for programs to store the results of their computations on external media. The external input-output units were extremely slow, and these waiting periods were taking a (relatively) high toll on the system efficiency.

Given that many systems of the time were loading several programs into memory, the next step in operating system design was a system that would switch control to another program whenever an executing program had to stop and wait on an input/output device. In this way, the processor could be in more or less continual use, and this would result in greatly increased system efficiency. It would, of course, also require a much more complex operating system to accomplish this.

Naturally, when an I/O operation finishes, its associated program will have the data available that it needs to continue executing, and the operating system should identify the program as ready to execute when some running program either finishes or requests an I/O operation. All of this requires a system that can detect I/O operation completions, identify which paused programs were associated with these I/O operations, and return that program to the "waiting" list of programs ready to continue executing. It was to support these kinds of capabilities that interrupt processing was developed. It is interrupt processing that allows programs to return control to the OS when pausing to wait out an I/O operation (or when terminating.)

1.2.4.1 Processes

It was becoming common for programs to be designed having shorter relatively independent subdivisions.

This was especially true of operating systems. Operating systems, having become extremely complex systems, were being subdivided into subprograms.

For example, one subprogram might be used to submit requests for data from external media, another might transfer control to a "waiting" program, when an executing program has paused, and still another might place a "paused" program back into the waiting queue when its I/O operation has completed.

Operating systems were not the only complex programs/systems in the computer science universe, and the technique of dividing complex programs into smaller simpler subdivisions was becoming pervasive. It became common, then to speak of the OS as dealing with (and consisting of) *processes*, rather than *programs*.

A *process* can be defined as an entity that can be assigned to, and executed on, a processor. It is a unit of activity characterized by a single sequential thread[2] of execution, a current state, and an associated set of system resources.

A process contains three components: *executable code*, *the associated data* needed by the process (variables, work space, buffers, etc.) and the *execution context* (or "process state") of the program. The execution context is essential because it is the internal data by which the OS is able to supervise and control the process. The execution context includes the contents of the various process registers, as well as other information such as the priority of the process and its state (waiting to execute or paused, if waiting on I/O, identification of the event, …)

1.2.5 Time Sharing

It was very quickly recognized that the system of loading several programs in memory at the same time and allowing another process to take over when an executing process has paused (i.e. *multiprogramming*) brought about a fundamental change in the way that the performance of computer systems should be *evaluated*. Previously, when an executing program had to finish before

---

[2] A **thread** of execution is the smallest sequence of programmed instructions that can be managed independently by a scheduler. *Threads* differ from traditional *processes* in that:
- processes are typically independent, while a thread must exist as a subset of a process.
- processes carry considerably more state information than threads, whereas multiple threads within a process share process state as well as memory and other resources
- processes have separate address spaces, whereas threads share their address space
- processes interact only through system-provided inter-process communication mechanisms

another could start, the emphasis was entirely on getting each program to execute as fast as possible[3]. Now, however, with systems in which several programs could be sharing access to the processor, the emphasis (at least in some installations) switched from how fast *one* program could be processed to how many programs could be finished in a given time period. At the same time, the price of memory (RAM) was coming down, which facilitated systems with greater numbers of simultaneous programs.

With this change of emphasis, came the realization that "compute bound" programs (programs that seldom stopped to wait for I/O) tended to block the progress of other programs in the system. They could take control of the CPU for long periods of time without relinquishing it. I/O bound programs, on the other hand, would spend much of their time waiting for data transfer, and would use relatively little of the processor time. A computing system could support a larger number of I/O bound programs since, at any given time, many (probably most) of them would be in a suspended state and placing no load on the CPU.

In order to permit the I/O bound programs to proceed (once their blocking I/O operation had finished) it was found to be desirable to force the compute bound programs to relinquish control at regular intervals, and the system of "time slicing" was developed. When a process would begin executing, it would be assigned a "slice[4]" of time, during which it would be allowed to use the processor. If the process paused for an I/O operation, it would be placed in a "suspended" state, another waiting process would be awarded a time slice and allowed to proceed. When the I/O operation finished, the state of the suspended process would be changed to "waiting" and it would be placed in the list of processes waiting their turn for cpu time. In the event that a slice of time expired before the process paused for I/O (or for any other reason) the process would be interrupted, placed in a waiting state, the next process in the waiting list would be assigned a time slice and the interrupted process would be placed in the waiting list.

1.2.6 Interactive Multiuser Systems

It soon occurred to system designers (and purchasers) that it might be convenient to allow users to interact directly with the computer systems, rather than requiring them to physically hand over their programs (usually as packs of punched cards) to operators, and then wait for the programs to produce printed output that would then be handed back (probably the following morning.) At this time, teletype terminals were becoming relatively common, and provided a convenient means

---

[3]   The related problem of choosing programs that would execute quickly was seen as more political (in the sense of *office politics*) than technical.

[4]   Sometimes referred to as a "quantum"

for communication with computing systems. Such direct human interactions would tend to be quite I/O intensive since human response time is *much* slower than that of computers. Even a relatively large number of simultaneous "online" users would add relatively little to the cpu load, since an interactive program would spend much of its time in a paused state, waiting for a user to do something.

Interactive support systems were designed to allow users to write, compile, and execute their own programs online from computer terminals. This in turn helped to lower operational costs, since fewer personnel were needed to load programs and data (users were doing that themselves from their terminals.) It also opened computer access to a much wider group of people.

1.2.7 Systems with Virtual Memory

Interactive multiuser systems were creating situations with larger and larger numbers of programs sitting in a suspended state waiting for user input, and, at the same time, random access external storage systems (hard disks) were being developed with access times that, although terribly slow from the point of view of the cpu, were essentially instantaneous from the point of view of a human user. These external storage systems were (and are) much cheaper than RAM. It seemed obvious that even larger numbers of users could be accommodated (on systems of the same price) if their suspended programs could be stored on disk, rather than occupying (relatively) expensive RAM, until ready to resume execution.

Virtual memory systems were developed to transfer to disk contents of memory that were unlikely to be referenced in the immediate future. These might include programs that were paused waiting on I/O but could also include subsections of executing programs, if these sections did not involve code or data likely to be referenced soon.

Of course the management of these virtual memory systems required operating systems even more complex than earlier systems. These OS's now had to identify which programs and/or program segments would not be referenced immediately and keep track of where on disk the segments were stored. They needed the ability to retrieve these programs and/or segments and to locate space in RAM to copy them after retrieval. This had to be done in a way that the segments would be compatible with any other segments already in RAM and it had to be done relatively quickly (at least from the point of view of online users.)

Virtual memory can be an effective strategy for dividing large programs largely because of the "Principle of Locality".

1.2.7.1 Principle of Locality

This principle states that memory references by the processor tend to cluster.

Most programs include sections of sequential code and these command codes will be close together (one after another) in memory. Programs frequently include *iterations* (sections of code that, once initiated, are executed repeatedly.) Data is often stored as arrays, which are stored sequentially, and programs tend to reference multiple entries in a given array. As a general rule, then, if a program references a given location in RAM, it is likely that the next few memory references will also be to locations close to that same location.

If, for a reasonable period of time, none of the cells in a particular section of memory have been referenced, then it is likely that the next several memory references will continue to be to cells in some different section of memory, and so, if the "not to be referenced" section were to be swapped out, the system performance would not be affected (at least for a while.)

Locality of reference for user software has recently weakened somewhat. This is mostly attributed to the spread of object-oriented programming, which tends to make use of large numbers of small functions, and the increased use of sophisticated data structures like trees and hash tables that tend to result in chaotic memory reference patterns.

1.2.8 Systems with Cache Memory

It did not take systems designers long to figure out that there could be benefits applying the principle of locality in the other direction as well.

If a CPU references a cell in a given section of RAM, then it is likely that the next few memory references will also be to cells in that same section.

New technology was being developed that permitted the creation of RAM that supported much faster memory references. Unfortunately, this newer faster RAM was also much more expensive, used more power and produced more heat. It was not cost effective to build computers in which the high speed technology was used for *all* of the RAM, but it *was* possible to include a relatively small amount of high speed RAM (called a cache.) When the processor referenced a location in normal RAM, the section of memory containing that cell could be copied into the cache, and, by the principle of locality, the next several memory references would probably be made using the high speed RAM in the cache, rather than regular RAM. In this way, although only a small amount of memory used high speed technology, most of the CPU operations *would* be executed using that memory. Of course, in systems with cache memory, the operating system has the additional responsibility of keeping track of which memory sections are duplicated in cache, which sections have been referenced recently, and which cache cells have had their contents modified (and must be copied back to regular RAM before being replaced by more recently accessed memory sections.)

1.2.9 Systems with Disk Caches

Many programs do a great deal of disk I/O, saving data to disk and/or retrieving data from disk. The progress of such programs is very much impeded by the relatively slow (compared to CPU operations and RAM access) disk access times. Of course, the principle of locality also applies to disk access, so, in order to speed the progress of these I/O bound programs, systems similar to memory cache systems were designed that retain copies of recently referenced sections of disk in RAM where they could be referenced more quickly.

1.2.10 Personal Computers

Early computers were large and expensive, and, as time passed, computers became larger, more complex and even more expensive, but the 1960's saw a segmentation of the computer market. Less complex and less expensive computers (minicomputers) entered the market. This division of the market did not, however, have an important effect on operating system development until the mid 1970's when the invention of the microprocessor made it possible for computer companies to begin marketing personal computers to individuals.

A **microprocessor** is a computer processor that incorporates all the functions of a CPU on a single integrated circuit (IC). The integration of a whole CPU onto a single chip reduces the cost of processing power and increases efficiency. Integrated circuit processors are produced in large numbers by highly automated processes, resulting in a low per-unit cost. Single-chip processors increase reliability because there are many fewer electrical connections to fail. Before microprocessors, small computers had been built using racks of circuit boards with many medium- and small-scale integrated circuits. Microprocessors combined this into one large-scale IC.

Texas Instruments TMS1000.

Intel 4004.

Continued increases in microprocessor capacity have since rendered other forms of computers almost completely obsolete, with one or more microprocessors used in everything from the smallest embedded systems and handheld devices to the largest mainframes and supercomputers.

Motorola 6800.

Before the introduction of the personal computer, all computer systems were operated by trained specialists, but, of course, this was generally not the case with the personal computers. The advent of personal computers, then, made the user interface a much higher priority in operating system design. Obviously, systems that were easier to use (more "user friendly") could be marketed to a much wider audience. The earliest personal computer operating systems were running on systems with very limited resources (small amounts of RAM, external storage that was slow and had limited capacity, relatively slow processors.) The earliest personal computer operating systems tended to feature menu driven interfaces that were relatively simple to implement and required relatively few resources, as well as being easy for inexperienced users to understand and use.

Later, the personal computers became larger and faster, and started to come with bigger and faster external storage systems and larger displays. More complex interface systems (GUI's) were developed that made the personal computer even easier for untrained people to use.

1.2.11 [ii]Multiprocessors

In their never-ending search for ways to make computers work even faster, designers began creating multiprocessors, that is, chips which contain multiple processors[5], with the idea that several cores could process different processes simultaneously, and thus process their data several times faster than could a single processor.

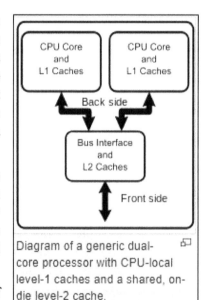

Diagram of a generic dual-core processor with CPU-local level-1 caches and a shared, on-die level-2 cache.

This, of course, requires that some part of the system be capable of identifying which processes could be processed simultaneously and which were inherently sequential (one having to complete before the next could begin.)

Multiprocessor systems have a number of advantages over single processor systems. Principal among them, of course, is the capability of executing (at least some) programs faster, but, in addition, there is the factor that they are more robust. If

---

[5] referred to as "cores" A **multi-core processor** is a single computing component with two or more independent processing units called cores, which read and execute program instructions

one processor fails, the system can continue functioning (although probably at a somewhat reduced efficiency.)

Multiprocessor systems have the disadvantage of requiring a much more complex operating system (among other things, capable of identifying the processes that can be executed simultaneously and avoiding deadlock situations.) These operating systems will require more memory and take more time to run than simpler purely sequential systems. Thus for a purely sequential problem, a multiprocessor system might end up being slower than a system with only one processor (a processor as fast as any one of the multiple processors in the multiprocessor, of course.)

1.2.12 Smart Phones

With the arrival, and wide public acceptance of the smart phone (a combination of cell phone and computer) came a different set of priorities and constraints for operating systems.

Smart phones have relatively small displays

Most of their users have no formal training and limited experience in the use of computers.

There was also an obvious need for an efficient interface with the telephone's communications system.

There are many more smart phones than any other kind of computer[6], and so the operating systems on smart phones constitute the vast majority of the operating systems currently extant.

1.2.13 Embedded Systems

Computing system hardware has become quite cheap and is now commonly built into other products (household appliances, automobiles, pacemakers, …)

The embedded systems are designed for specific functions, and their operating systems are very different from the systems for general purpose computers, and, indeed, from one another. An embedded system's key feature is dedication to specific functions, but they often require strong general-purpose processors. For example, router and switch systems are embedded systems. Embedded routers function more efficiently than OS-based computers for routing functionalities.

Commercial embedded systems range from digital watches and MP3 players to giant routers and switches. Complexities vary from single processor chips to advanced units with multiple processing chips

---

[6] General purpose computer, i.e. computer operated directly by a human user. There are probably many more *embedded* computers than smartphones.

1.3   Chapter 1 Questions:

  1.3.1   True-False

    1.3.1.1   The primary function of a computing system is to process data.

    1.3.1.2   ROM is "volatile", which means it loses its contents when the computer is shut down

    1.3.1.3   Operating Systems are among the most complex pieces of software ever developed

    1.3.1.4   Portability and ease of use were the primary motivating factors in most of the early computer development.

    1.3.1.5   On the earliest computers there was nothing even remotely resembling what we would call an operating system

    1.3.1.6   The development of sophisticated I/O device interfaces allowed programs to return control to the OS when pausing to wait out an I/O operation (or when terminating.)

    1.3.1.7   "compute bound" programs (programs that seldom stop to wait for I/O) tend to block the progress of other programs in systems without time slicing.

    1.3.1.8   "external storage systems were (and are) much cheaper than RAM

    1.3.1.9   The 1960's saw a segmentation of the computer market as less complex and less expensive computers (minicomputers) entered the market. This division of the market had an immediate impact on operating system development

    1.3.1.10   The advent of personal computers, made the user interface a much higher priority in operating system design

    1.3.1.11   With the arrival, and wide public acceptance of the smart phone (a combination of cell phone and computer) manufacturers were able to use simpler user interfaces since few of the phones were being used for complex programming tasks

    1.3.1.12   Embedded systems are designed for specific functions, and their operating systems are very different from the systems for general purpose computers, and, indeed, from one another.

    1.3.1.13   An embedded system's key feature is dedication to specific functions, and for this reason they normally require specialized processors.

1.3.2 Multiple Choice

1.3.2.1 The operating system is an important part of the software of any computer system. An operating system has several functions. One of these functions would be:
a. controlling access to the processor(s)
b. providing a set of services to users of the system (determining how they can interact with the system)
c. managing system hardware components
d. all of the above
e. none of the above

1.3.2.3 The first primitive operating systems, which were developed in the mid-_____ were small supervisor programs that provided basic I/O operations (such as control of punch card and/or tape readers and printers.)
a. 1940s
b. 1950s
c. 1960s
d. 1970s
e. none of the above

1.3.2.4 Locality of reference for user software has recently weakened somewhat. This is mostly attributed to the spread of
a. object oriented programming
b. trees as data structures
c. hash tables
d. all of the above
e. none of the above

1.3.2.5 The 1960's saw a segmentation of the computer market as less complex and less expensive computers (_____) entered the market.
a. minicomputers
b. personal computers
c. microcomputers
d. smartphones
e. none of the above

1.3.2.6 The _____'s saw a segmentation of the computer market as less complex and less expensive computers (minicomputers) entered the market.
a. 1960
b. 1970
c. 1980
d. 1990
e. none of the above

1.3.3 Completion

1.3.3.1 A processing unit (also referred to as a _____) controls the operation of the computer and performs the data processing functions. It executes the commands that result in the processing of the system's data.

1.3.3.2 Common input devices are keyboards and _____ devices such as trackballs or mice

1.3.3.3 The operating system's I/O _____ provide control of movement of data between the computer and external environments, including: storage devices, communications equipment and other I/O devices

1.3.3.4 An Operating System is a program, or collection of programs, that manages the _____ of a computer system

1.3.3.5 The first primitive operating systems, which were developed in the mid-1950s were small *supervisor programs* that provided basic I/O operations (such as control of punch card and/or tape readers and printers.) The systems using these were described as _____ processing systems.

1.3.3.6 The inclusion of an operating system adds _____ to the system. Operating system programs occupy space in memory and they take time to execute, but are not, themselves, application programs.

1.3.3.7 A process contains three components: ***executable code***, ***the associated data*** needed by the process and the ***execution*** _____ (or "process state") of the program.

1.3.3.8 _____ *memory* systems were developed to transfer to disk contents of memory that were unlikely to be referenced in the immediate future.

1.3.3.9 It was not cost effective to build computers in which the high speed technology was used for *all* of the RAM, but it *was* possible to include a relatively small amount of high speed RAM (called a (n) _____)

1.3.3.10 The earliest personal computer operating systems tended to feature _____ driven interfaces

1.3.3.11 As personal computers became larger and faster, more complex interface systems (_____ 's) were developed that made the personal computer easier for untrained people to use

2. Characteristics of Operating Systems

As stated earlier, a computing system requires a set of resources for the processing, moving and storing of data. [iii]Typical resources include the central processing unit (CPU), computer memory, file storage, input/output (I/O) devices, and network connections, as well as a system of buses to move data from one resource to another. An operating system manages these resources and provides interfaces[7] for coordination among them.

Thus, the OS is responsible for managing and coordinating the system resources, and, in addition, must provide interfaces for communication between:

users,

software,

hardware,

and peripheral devices.

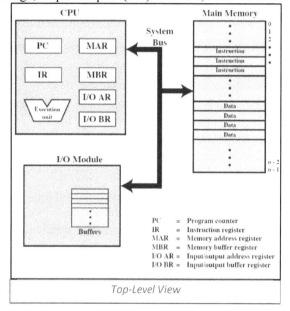

Top-Level View

For the earliest operating systems, the main priority in design of computing systems was efficiency/speed of execution and this was interpreted as how fast each single program could be processed. When systems were developed which could load more than one program at a time, the emphasis shifted, and a higher priority was given to the number of programs that could be executed in a given time period, and a lower priority to the time for an individual program/job.

Then, as computers became bigger and faster, and were being used in a greater variety of situations, other factors began to take on greater importance, factors such as:

convenience

ease of use

portability

stability

---

[7]   An **interface** is a shared boundary across which two or more separate components of a computer system exchange information.

security

While operating systems used on small devices may be relatively simple, popular operating systems for these devices (like Windows, OSX and Linux) provide drivers for a wide range of devices, as well as complex sophisticated user interfaces.

The core part of an operating system is its kernel.

The **kernel**[iv] is a computer program that is the core of a computer's operating system, with complete control over everything in the system. On most systems, it is one of the first programs loaded on start-up (after the bootloader). It handles the rest of start-up as well as input/output requests from software, translating them into data-processing instructions for the central processing unit. It handles memory and peripherals like keyboards, monitors, printers, and speakers.

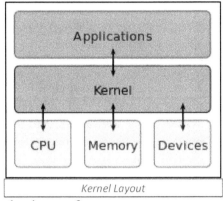

Kernel Layout

A kernel connects the application software to the hardware of a computer.

The critical code of the kernel is usually loaded into a separate area of memory, which is protected from access by application programs or other, less critical parts of the operating system. The kernel performs its tasks, such as running processes, managing hardware devices such as the hard disk, and handling interrupts, in this protected kernel space. In contrast, everything a user does is in user space: writing text in a text editor, running programs in a GUI, etc. This separation prevents user data and kernel data from interfering with each other and causing instability and slowness, as well as preventing malfunctioning application programs from crashing the entire operating system.

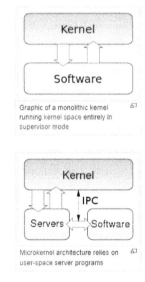

Graphic of a monolithic kernel running kernel space entirely in supervisor mode

When a process makes requests of the kernel, it is called a *system call*. Kernel designs differ in how they manage these system calls and resources. A monolithic kernel[v] runs all the operating system instructions in the same address space for speed. A microkernel runs most processes in user space, for modularity

Microkernel architecture relies on user-space server programs

Today, monolithic kernels[8] are the most popular. These kernels provide a way for different computer processes to send messages to each other, and they manage the RAM that stores program information. Most kernels also provide device drivers to control monitors, input devices, disk drives and other peripherals.

2.1 Characteristics of the Execution of an Operating System Program

In the end, an operating system consists of software (i.e. programs) and these programs, just like any other programs, must be processed by a CPU. They are just sequences of instructions that must be executed.

There are, however, a few ways in which operating system programs are atypical. For one thing, many operating system programs must have certain "executive privileges" that are not available to typical application programs. For another, many operating systems programs relinquish and regain control of the processor with greater frequency than just about any other kind of program. Finally, efficiency and reliability are much more important in the design of an operating system than they are in the design of any other kind of program.

[vi]2.1.1 Some OS Programs have Executive Privileges

There are some activities that common application programs should not be allowed to perform and areas of memory that they should not be allowed to access. Many of the operating system modules, however, are required to execute instructions that applications programs cannot execute, and some modules must

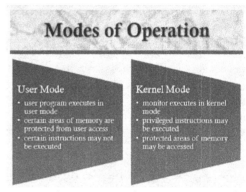

reference memory areas forbidden to normal programs (they can operate in "kernel space" rather than "user space".)

---

8   A **monolithic kernel** is an operating system architecture in which the entire operating system is working in "kernel space" and is alone in supervisor mode. The monolithic model differs from other operating system architectures (such as the microkernel architecture) in that it alone defines a high-level virtual interface over computer hardware. A set of primitives or system calls implement all operating system services such as process management, concurrency, and memory management. Device drivers can be added to the kernel as modules (see chapter 3.)

2.1.2 Some OS Programs must Relinquish and Regain Control very Frequently

Most modern computing systems are multiprocessing systems. When an application program begins executing, it is the operating system that transfers control to it, and, in doing so, relinquishes its control. At some point, the application program must stop, possibly because it has finished, possibly because it paused for an I/O operation, or possibly because it finished its time slice. For whatever reason, the operating system regains control. The OS program called the *monitor* begins to execute. The monitor identifies a process that would be appropriate to execute and passes CPU control to that process.

Application programs can (and often do) relinquish control, only to take up execution later. Few, however, will ever do so as frequently as does any operating system monitor.

2.1.3 OS Programs Must Be Efficient

Very few programs execute as frequently as the operating system programs, and, hence, any inefficiencies in their execution will tend to slow the system much more than would inefficiencies in a program of another type. In particular, it is essential that the manner in which control of the cpu is transferred be efficient, since this activity occurs with great frequency (see 2.1.2 above) and any inefficiencies in the process would result in significant slowdowns of system operation.

2.1.4 OS Programs Must Be Reliable

As noted above, operating system programs execute very frequently. Since they execute frequently, any programming errors in them will occur more frequently than will errors in other types of programs. In addition, other programs depend on OS programs for their functioning, and so errors will affect the execution of the other programs too, and not just the individual OS program containing the error. Finally, OS programs are permitted wider range of memory access than are common programs and they can use commands not allowed in common application programs. An error in an OS program would have much greater potential for doing serious damage than would a similar error in a normal application program.

2.1.5 Some OS Programs cannot be Swapped Out to Virtual Memory

The monitor/kernel handles all interrupts. An interrupt can occur at any time, and so the monitor must be resident in RAM at all times.

2.2 An OS Must Function as a Resource Manager

Application programs are (generally) resource *users*. The operating system, on the other hand, functions as the resource *manager*[vii].

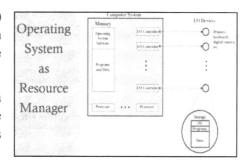

A computing system will typically have a limited number of resources[9], and quite often there will be several processes running concurrently.

When several processes are executing simultaneously, it is pretty much inevitable that two of them will attempt to access the same system resource at the same time. Many system resources can only be used by one process at a time, and so some control must be exercised over which process gets to use the resource. This is another of the responsibilities of the operating system Hence, there must be some system/policy established to govern how the system resources are to be allocated.

2.2.1 Factors in Resource Allocation Policy

Among the factors that must be considered in the design of resource allocation policies are: fairness, differential responsiveness and efficiency. Resources should also be allocated in a manner that avoids "deadlocks" and "starvation". These objectives are not necessarily mutually consistent, and systems will be designed to give some of the objectives greater priorities, depending on what kind of system they are for.

2.2.1.1 Fairness

Resources should be allocated in a way that all processes should have a reasonable expectation of obtaining the resources they need in a reasonable time.

Of course all operating systems should be "fair" in the above sense. An operating system should never permit "starvation" (see below) but "reasonable time" is subject to interpretation. What an online user would consider a reasonable time is not what would be considered reasonable for a batch job. What one user would consider "fair" is not necessarily what another user would consider "fair".

---

[9] Some examples of resources are processors, primary storage, peripherals, secondary storage, and files

2.2.1.2 Responsiveness

Resources should be allocated in a way that *online* users should have a reasonable expectation of system interaction in what an online user might consider a "reasonable"[10] time.

Again, "reasonable time" is subject to interpretation. and in many situations, and for certain kinds of processes, 24 hours might well be considered "reasonable", whereas on a personal computer or on a system whose users do most of their work online, today Kemeny and Kurtz's standard of 10 seconds would probably be considered very much excessive.

2.2.1.3 Efficiency

Resources should be allocated in a way that resources are utilized to their greatest degree possible.

This factor tends to be inconsistent with both fairness and responsiveness, and, if given too high a priority, could lead to "starvation". It does, however, have its place in system allocation policies, especially in design of OS's for systems with resources that are extremely expensive (supercomputers for example.)

2.2.1.4 Avoidance of Deadlock and Starvation

In resource allocation, the OS must deal with the most problematic kinds of conflicts. When concurrent processes compete for the same resources, it is quite possible that after a process has been allocated one resource, it might attempt to access a second resource. If that second resource has already been allocated to a second process, the first process must wait until the second process releases it. Then, however the second process might request access to the first resource and the second process will have to wait for the first process to release that resource. At this point, neither process can proceed. If neither process will release its resource until it has finished its task, then neither will be able to finish because each requires a resource that the other will not release. Such a situation is called a *deadlock[viii]*. Another, more subtle kind of problem

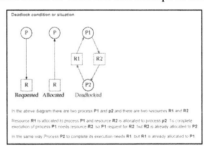

[10] When designing DTSS (the first successful large-scale time-sharing system to be implemented response time.) Kemeny and Kurtz are on record as identifying 10 seconds as the maximum response time

can occur in a busy system when a process needs a commonly used resource, but cannot access it because other, higher priority processes are continually using it. This kind of situation is called *starvation*.

Operating systems must be designed to identify potential deadlock and starvation situations and prevent them from occurring. If one of these situations does occur, the system must recognize the fact and deal with it (quickly if at all possible.)

2.3   Chapter 2 Questions

2.3.1   True-False

2.3.1.1 Because of the limited memory available, operating systems used on small devices are necessarily quite complex

2.3.1.2 A kernel connects the application software to the hardware of a computer

2.3.1.3 The critical code of the kernel is usually loaded into a separate area of memory, which is protected from access by application programs or other, less critical parts of the operating system.

2.3.1.4 Kernel designs differ in how they manage these system calls and resources. A monolithic kernel runs all the operating system instructions in the same address space for speed. A microkernel runs most processes in user space, for modularity. Today, microkernels are the most popular.

2.3.1.5 The monolithic model differs from other operating system architectures in that it alone defines a high-level virtual interface over computer hardware

2.3.1.6 Because OS programs have more restrictions on the memory they can access than do application programs, an error in an OS program would have less potential for doing serious damage than would a similar error in a normal application program.

2.3.1.7 Among the factors that must be considered in the design of resource allocation policies are: fairness, differential responsiveness and efficiency. Resources should also be allocated in a manner that avoids "deadlocks" and "starvation". These objectives are not necessarily mutually consistent

2.3.1.8 Efficiency: Resources should be allocated in a way that resources are utilized to their greatest degree possible.
This factor tends to be inconsistent with both fairness and responsiveness

2.3.2   Multiple Choice

2.3.2.1 A computing system requires a set of resources for the _____ of data
    a.   processing
    b.   moving
    c.   storing
    d.   all of the above
    e.   none of the above

2.3.2.2 When a process makes requests of the kernel, it is called a _____
    a.   service request
    b.   system call
    c.   kernel call
    d.   core request
    e.   none of the above

2.3.2.3 Most modern computing systems are _____ systems
   a.   batch
   b.   application
   c.   multiprocessing
   d.   multiuser
   e.   none of the above

2.3.2.4 Resources should be allocated in a way that all processes should have a reasonable expectation of obtaining the resources they need in a reasonable time. This factor that must be considered in the design of resource allocation policies is the factor of _____
   a.   fairness
   b.   differential responsiveness
   c.   efficiency
   d.   all of the above
   e.   none of the above

2.3.3   Completion

2.3.3.1 A computing system requires a set of _____ for the processing, moving and storing of data

2.3.3.2 A(n) _____ is a shared boundary across which two or more separate components of a computer system exchange information

2.3.3.3 The _____ is a computer program that is the core of a computer's operating system, with complete control over everything in the system.

2.3.3.4 Kernel designs differ in how they manage these system calls and resources. A(n) _____ kernel runs all the operating system instructions in the same address space for speed.

2.3.3.5 A(n) _____ **kernel** is an operating system architecture in which the entire operating system is working in "kernel space" and is alone in supervisor mode

2.3.3.6 When an application program relinquishes control, the OS program called the _____ begins to execute.

2.3.3.7 Application programs are (generally) resource *users*. The operating system, on the other hand, functions as the resource _____

2.3.3.8 When a process needs a commonly used resource, but cannot access it because other, higher priority processes are continually using it, this kind of situation is called _____.

3. Relationships of the Operating System Modules

Practically speaking, division of the system into dynamically loadable modules is a very flexible way of handling an operating system image at runtime (as opposed to rebooting with a different operating system image whenever additional functionality might be required.) The separation of the OS into distinct modules with specific responsibilities allows for easy extension/upgrading of the operating systems' capabilities as required. Dynamically loadable modules incur a small overhead when compared to building all conceivable functionality into the operating system image.

Loading modules dynamically (as-needed) helps to keep the amount of code running in kernel space to a minimum. It will reduce operating system footprint to optimum size (especially important for embedded devices or those with limited hardware resources.) Unloaded modules need not be stored in (possibly scarce and/or expensive) random access memory.

An operating system has a number of responsibilities and must perform many varied functions. It is only reasonable that these different activities be executed by separate programs/modules, some of which may be permanently resident (part of the kernel) and some may be dynamically loadable (reducing the kernel footprint, as mentioned earlier.) This type of organization simplifies (somewhat) the design of what is (as mentioned earlier) one of the most complex types of programs in the history of the industry. It also simplifies updating the OS, since an update may involve modification of only a portion of the programming (i.e. one or two modules) at any one time.

Among the modules involved in an operating system would be:

Process management module.

Memory management module:

I/O modules:

3.1 *Process management module*:

The process management module controls which processes are to be allocated for a processor to execute. The process management module includes small processes/programs for switching the processor from one process to another (i.e. for transferring "*control*" from one process to another.)

3.1.1 What is a Process

Recall from 1.2.4.1, a process can be defined as an entity that can be assigned to, and executed by, a processor. It is a unit of activity characterized by having a single sequential thread of execution, a current state, and an associated set of system resources.

A process contains three components: *executable code*, *the associated data* needed by the process (variables, work space, buffers, etc.) and the *execution context* (or "process state") of the program.

When the processor begins to execute program code, the code must be associated with some entity characterized as a *process*[ix].

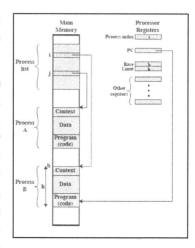

While the program/process is executing, the process can be uniquely characterized by a number of elements, including: *identifier, state, priority, program counter, memory pointers, context data, I/O status information* and *accounting by the processor.* There will be a *Process Control Block (PCB)*[x] which contains these process elements and it is the process control block that makes it possible to interrupt a running process and later resume execution as if the interruption had not occurred. This *PCB* is created and managed by the operating system and is a key tool that allows support for both interrupt processing and multiple concurrent processes.

One of the activities of the process manager is that of handling the removal of a running process from a CPU and the selection of another process for the CPU to begin executing. It is best that this selection process (*process scheduling*) be made on the basis of some strategy. Process scheduling is an essential part of a multiprogramming operating system.

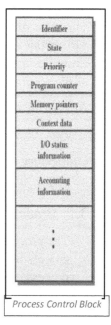

Process Control Block

The OS maintains all PCBs in Process Scheduling Queues. The system will maintain a separate queue for each of the process states and PCBs of all processes in the same execution state are placed in the same queue. When the state of a process is changed, its PCB is unlinked from its current queue and linked into its new state queue.

The behavior of an individual process can be traced by listing the sequence of instructions that the process executes. The behavior of the processor can be characterized by showing how the traces of the various processes are interleaved.

There are several different state models.

3.1.1.1   Process States: 2 State Model[xi]

The simplest of the models involves only two states. "Running" and "Not-Running".

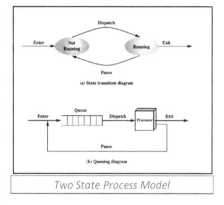

In a system using this model, a process is only created if it can begin executing immediately. Processes are only entered into the system when they can be entered in the "Running" state.

In this system, when a running process is interrupted, it is transferred to the

Two State Process Model

"Not-Running" queue, unless it finished running or aborted. In either of these two cases, the process would be discarded, and a process would be selected from the "Not-Running" queue to execute.

3.1.1.2   Process States: 5 State Model[xii]

Possibly the most commonly used state model is the 5 state model:

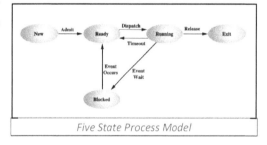

Five-State Process Model:
A process may be in one of five distinct states:
1. ***Created/New***: The process has been

Five State Process Model

   loaded in memory but has not yet been entered into either the "waiting" queue of processes ready to be executed or the list of "Blocked" processes waiting for some event to free them for execution.
2. ***Ready:*** The process is in memory and is in the "waiting" queue, waiting to be assigned to a processor to be executed
3. ***Running:*** The process is being executed by a processor.
4. ***Blocked:*** The process is waiting for some event (like: I/O completion, allocation of some resource, etc.)
5. ***Exit:*** The process has already finished its execution.

3.1.1.3   Process States: 7 State Model[xiii]

Two additional states are available for processes in systems that support virtual memory. In both of these states, processes are "stored" on secondary memory (typically a hard disk).

Seven State Process Model

Swapped out and waiting

(Also called **suspended and waiting**.) In systems that support virtual memory, a process may be swapped out, that is, removed from main memory and placed on external storage by the scheduler. From here the process may be swapped back into the waiting state.

Swapped out and blocked

(Also called **suspended and blocked**.) Processes that are blocked may also be swapped out. In this event the process is both swapped out and blocked, and may be swapped back in again under the same circumstances as a swapped out and waiting process (although in this case, the process will move to the blocked state, and may still be waiting for a resource to become available).

3.1.1.4   Changing Process States

There are a number of reasons that a "Running" process might stop:

its time slice might have finished;

it might have stopped to wait for an I/O operation to complete;

it might have stopped to issue a request to spawn a new process;

it might have finished its task;

it might have been preempted by a higher priority process (a notification that an I/O operation has finished would be a common example);

it might have reached a point where it needs some additional system resource;

it might have stopped for some other reason.

For whatever reason, if the running process stops, control must be transferred to another process. The CPU cannot just stop operating, it must execute SOME instruction.

When a process stops, an interrupt will be generated. It is possible that the process was stopped by an externally generated interrupt. It is also possible that the process itself generated the interrupt (signaling an I/O request or termination of its task.) The interrupt will include information needed for the system to determine what to do next. The process/program that starts executing whenever an interrupt occurs is the *system monitor*. The monitor, then, based on what kind of interrupt activated it, will choose another (appropriate) process and set the processor to executing that process.

If the original process stopped because its time slice expired, the monitor will choose a process that will change the state of the original process from "R*unning*" to "W*aiting*", put it in the queue of waiting processes, choose another process from the "*waiting*" queue, change the state of that process to "R*unning*" and transfer control to it.

If the stopping of the original process was because it requested some I/O operation, then the monitor/kernel must change the state of the process to *"Blocked", put it in the list of "Blocked" processes,* and start the I/O module process for dealing with this kind of I/O request. The actual I/O operation will normally be done by equipment not under direct control of the CPU (I/O operations tend to be much slower than those controlled by a CPU, and so would slow the computer to an inacceptable degree if handled directly.) The process from I/O module will start the I/O equipment running and return control to the monitor. The monitor will then select a process from the "*waiting*" queue, set its state to "running" and start it executing.

On occasion, a running process will need to create (and execute) another (new) process. The procedure, in this case, is rather similar to that of an I/O request. In this case however instead of using a process from the I/O module, the monitor will choose a "*new process creation process*" from the process management module. It will create the new process (and deal with its state and queue position) and return control to the monitor so that it can select a process from the waiting queue.

If a process finishes its task, it will issue the appropriate interrupt, and, in response, the kernel will initiate the appropriate "*process termination process*" from the process management module. This process will reclaim the process resources and return control to the monitor so that it can select a process from the waiting queue.

If the I/O system completes an operation it will issue an interrupt. The monitor will identify the process that requested the original I/O operation, change the state of that process from *blocked* to *waiting*, put it in the waiting queue and return control to the process that had been running when the I/O interrupt occurred.

31

In general, whenever an interrupt occurs, control transfers to the monitor. The monitor determines what kind of interrupt caused it to start running and takes appropriate action to deal with that interrupt.

3.1.2   Process Scheduling

Schedulers are special system software which handle process scheduling in various ways. Their main task is to select the jobs to be submitted into the system and to decide which process to run. Schedulers are of three types:

Short-Term Schedulers; Long-Term Schedulers; Medium-Term Schedulers:

3.1.2.1   Short-Term Schedulers

Short-Term Schedulers (aka *CPU schedulers*) have, as their main objective to increase system performance (in accordance with some chosen set of criteria.) A CPU scheduler selects a process from among the processes in the "waiting" queue and allocates CPU to it.

3.1.2.2   Long Term Schedulers

Long Term Schedulers are also called *job schedulers*. A long term scheduler determines which programs are admitted to the system for processing. It selects processes from the "created" queue, loads them into memory for execution and inserts them into either the "waiting" or "blocked" queue as appropriate.

The primary objective of the job scheduler is to provide a balanced mix of jobs, such as I/O bound and processor bound. It also controls the degree of multiprogramming. For the degree of multiprogramming to be stable, the average rate of process creation must be equal to the average departure rate of processes leaving the system.

On some systems, the long-term scheduler may not be available or minimal. Time-sharing operating systems will have no long term scheduler. On these systems, a process automatically changes state from new to ready.

3.1.2.3   Medium Term Scheduler

Medium-term scheduling is a part of the virtual memory process. It removes the processes from the memory, and returns them to memory, as needed.

A running process may become suspended if it makes an I/O request. A suspended process cannot make any progress towards completion. In this condition, to remove the process from memory and make space for other processes, the suspended process is moved to the secondary storage. This process is called swapping, and the process is said to be swapped out or rolled out.

A medium-term scheduler identifies which processes to swap out and swap back in.

3.2 Memory management module:

memory management is the function responsible for managing the computer's primary memory. The memory management function keeps track of the status of each memory location, either *allocated* or *free*. It determines how memory is allocated among competing processes. It decides which process gets memory, when it gets it, how much it gets, and what memory it is to get. When memory is to be allocated, memory management determines which memory locations will be assigned. It also tracks when memory is freed or *deallocated* and updates the status of those memory locations.

At its core, then, the memory manager has the task of allocating memory to each job/process to be executed and of reclaiming the memory whenever a process completes, or, for some other reason, releases memory.

In any system, an application program must be restricted as to what areas of memory it can access. Even in the simplest single user single process batch systems, the operating system code must be protected from being overwritten by an application process, so the "memory allocation" referred to above, implies some form of system control over the memory allocated to, and used by, the processes.

In multiprogramming systems, decisions must be made concerning where a given program will be loaded into memory and, once loaded, what areas it can access. Then, these limitations must be enforced.

The memory manager will check the validity of each request for memory space, and, if it is a legal request, will allocate a section of unused RAM. The manager maintains a table keeping track of what sections are allocated to what. Note that this is complicated by the fact that, although the memory used by distinct processes will normally be nonoverlapping, there will be situations (buffers used in synchronization of concurrent processes) in which two processes might need to reference the same memory. It is the responsibility of the memory management system to keep track of and enforce the process reference rights.

In systems supporting virtual memory and/or cache memory, the memory manager will typically set up tables to keep track of which sections of memory are allocated to which processes, which blocks are associated with which blocks of cache, which process pages have been swapped out to which pages of virtual memory (and will issue commands to the I/O system to retrieve any virtual page, in the event that a process should reference something in it.)

3.3 I/O Module

The I/O Module is a system for exchanging data between processors and external I/O devices.

3.3.1 Types of I/O modules

There are several types of I/O module. A few of the most common are described below:

3.3.1.1 Programmed I/O

Programmed I/O is the simplest I/O technique for exchanging data between a processor and an external device.

With *Programmed I/O*, the processor executes a program that takes the direct control of I/O operation. The processor issues a command to the I/O device and waits until the operation is complete. The processor will periodically check the status of I/O module until it finds that the operation has completed.

3.3.1.2 Interrupt-driven I/O

Interrupt driven I/O has many features in common with Programmed I/O, but with this technique, the processor does not stop and wait for the I/O operation to complete. Instead, after issuing a command to an I/O device controller, it continues on, to process other tasks. When the I/O operation has finished, the I/O device will issue an interrupt and the processor will pause its operations and process the I/O interrupt.

3.3.1.3 DMA I/O

[xiv]DMA is an acronym for *Direct Memory Access*.
DMA I/O modules exchange data directly between memory and I/O devices without any involvement of a CPU.

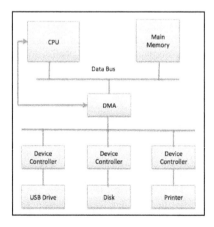

DMA I/O produces fast data transfer rates because there is no interference by CPU's.

With DMA, the CPU first initiates the transfer, issuing commands to the DMA controller, identifying devices, and memory buffer in RAM to be used. Then it goes on with other operations while the data transfer is in progress. It finally receives an **interrupt** from the DMA controller when the data transfer operation is done. This feature is especially useful in situations where the CPU cannot keep up with the rate of data transfer, or when the CPU needs to perform work while waiting for a relatively slow I/O data transfer. Many hardware systems use DMA, including **disk drive** controllers, **graphics cards**, **network cards** and **sound cards**.

DMA I/O differs from interrupt driven I/O in that with interrupt driven I/O, the CPU must deal with the device controller directly, copying data into or out of the controller, whereas with DMA I/O, the DMA controller does all the data transfer into or out of RAM.

3.3.2 I/O module Functions: [11]

The I/O module is responsible for moving data between the computer and external environments, (external peripheral devices.)

External devices generally have characteristics very different from those of internal memory (different response rates, different word sizes, …) so some form of interface is required between these devices and computer memory (so that the programs executing on a CPU can have some way to interact with the external devices.)

An I/O module (a device manager) manages communication with peripheral devices. It must balance supply and demand, and enforce policies dictated by device characteristics, as well as system load situations and local system priorities.

The primary functions and responsibilities of an I/O module would be:

Control and timing

Processor communication

Device communication

Data buffering

Error detection

3.3.2.1 Control and Timing:

When transferring data to or from RAM, communication with the external environment will generally use the same data buses that are used in the execution of normal programs. Of course, I/O transfer cannot take place at

---

[11] This section is taken largely from "Computer Organization and Architecture Designing for Performance" by William Stallings

the same time that the CPU is moving data to or from RAM as part of its program execution. An I/O control unit must transfer data from a buffer to a device or from a device to a buffer only at a time when the processor(s) will not be moving data to or from locations in RAM.

3.3.2.2 Processor Communication

Processor communication involves:

Command Decoding: The I/O module receives commands from the processor (on the control bus) identifies the commands and any parameters

Data: Data to be stored on external device, or data retrieved from external device are exchanged between I/O module and processor using data bus.

Status reporting: I/O module reports on state (READY, BUSY, ERROR) so that processor (process doing I/O) can determine whether/when to send/receive another unit of data.

Address recognition: I/O module will often control more than one external device and so the module must recognize a unique address for each of the devices with which it interfaces.

3.3.2.3 Device communication

The I/O module interfaces with and controls external data storage devices. It must, then be able to:

send commands to each device

determine the status of any device

send or receive data to/from each device

3.3.2.4 Data Buffering

The data transfer rate in and out of main memory will in general be very different from that of an external device. (Most of these devices are much slower, but a few are much faster.) They also tend to send and receive data in standardized amounts (one byte at a time, one word at a time, one page at a time, etc.) and the input sizes do not necessarily match the output sizes (the processor might be sending data one byte at a time, but the hard disk uses data a sector of 512 bytes at a time.)

The I/O module must receive input data and store it until there is a sufficient amount and the receiving unit is ready to receive it.

3.3.2.5 Error Detection

I/O Modules are often responsible for error detection and subsequent reports of errors so that the system might deal with them. Data transmission and storage usually incorporate some kind of error detection strategies to identify when and (if possible) what kinds errors have occurred, either in storage or transmission. These detection strategies often involve parity bits. For more information, see chapter 8.

3.4 Chapter 3 Questions

3.4.1 True-False

3.4.1.1 One of the disadvantages of dynamically loadable modules is their relatively large I/O overhead when compared to building all conceivable functionality into the operating system image.

3.4.1.2 Different activities can be executed by separate programs/modules. Some of the modules may be permanently resident (part of the kernel) and some may be dynamically loadable.

3.4.1.3 The OS maintains all PCBs in the **Process Scheduling Queue (PSQ).**

3.4.1.4 If a running process stops, the CPU will pause until another process can be selected to receive control

3.4.1.5 There are several types of I/O module

3.4.1.6 Most external devices generally have characteristics very similar to those of internal memory

3.4.1.7 Communication with the external environment will generally use the same data buses that are used in the execution of normal programs

3.4.1.8 An I/O module will often control more than one external device and so the module must recognize a unique address for each of the devices with which it interfaces

3.4.1.9 Data transmission and storage usually incorporate some kind of error detection strategies to identify when and (if possible) what kinds errors have occurred, either in storage or transmission. These detection strategies often involve parity bits

3.4.2 Multiple Choice

3.4.2.1 Using dynamically loadable modules _____
    a.   helps to keep the amount of code running in kernel space to a minimum.
    b.   will reduce operating system footprint to optimum size
    c.   allows for easy extension/upgrading of the operating system
    d.   all of the above
    e.   none of the above

3.4.2.2 While the program/process is executing, the process can be uniquely characterized by a number of elements, including: *identifier, state, priority, program counter*, *memory pointers, context data, I/O status information* and *accounting by the processor.* There will be a _____ which contains these process elements
a. ***Process Assignment Block (PAB)***
b. ***Process Assignment Table (PAT)***
c. ***Process Control Block (PCB)***
d. ***Process Control Table (PCT)***
e. none of the above

3.4.2.3 Possibly the most commonly used state model is the _____ model
a. one state
b. two state
c. five state
d. seven state
e. none of the above

3.4.2.4 A(n) _____ scheduler has, as its main objective to increase system performance (in accordance with some chosen set of criteria.) It selects a process from among the processes in the "waiting" queue to be allocated a CPU
a. short term
b. long term
c. medium term
d. interrupt processing
e. none of the above

3.4.2.5 In systems with cache memory and/or virtual memory, the memory manager will typically set up _____ to keep track of which sections of memory are allocated to which processes, which are associated with sections of cache and which processes involve what kind of sections of virtual memory.
a. lists
b. queues
c. tables
d. stacks
e. none of the above

3.4.2.6 With _____ I/O the processor will periodically check the status of I/O module until it finds that the operation has completed.
a. Programmed
b. Interrupt Driven
c. DMA
d. Modular
e. none of the above

3.4.2.7 A hardware system that might use DMA would be a _____
  a.   disk drive controller
  b.   sound card
  c.   network card
  d.   all of the above
  e.   none of the above

3.4.3 Completion

3.4.3.1 Division of the system into dynamically loadable _____ is a very flexible way of handling an operating system image at runtime (as opposed to rebooting with a different operating system image whenever additional functionality might be required.)

3.4.3.2 A process is a unit of activity characterized by having a single sequential _____ of execution, a current state, and an associated set of system resources

3.4.3.3 A process is a unit of activity characterized by having a single sequential thread of execution, a current state, and an associated set of system _____

3.4.3.4 In a two state model system, processes are only entered into the system when they can be entered in the "_____" state

3.4.3.5 In a five (or seven) state model system, a process is said to be in the _____ state if it is in memory and is in the "waiting" queue, waiting to be assigned to a processor to be executed

3.4.3.6 When a process stops, a(n) _____ will be generated.

3.4.3.7 For the degree of _____ to be stable, the average rate of process creation must be equal to the average departure rate of processes leaving the system

3.4.3.8 The I/O Module is a system for exchanging data between processors and _____ I/O devices

3.4.3.9 DMA is an acronym for _____ *Memory Access*

3.4.3.10 External devices generally have characteristics very different from those of internal memory (different response rates, different word sizes, …) so some form of _____ is required between these devices and computer memory

4. Concurrent Processes and Synchronization, Deadlocks and Starvation

All modern operating systems have to deal with the problems of concurrent processes (processes dealing with things that are going on simultaneously.) Even the systems on the simplest single user personal computers must control the display on the monitor and deal with user input from keyboard and/or mouse concurrently with the execution of any of the user's application programs.

In fact, computing systems have evolved to where most modern systems involve more than one processor (are *multiprocessor* systems), and so, while older single processor systems can give the *impression* of concurrent processing (using time slicing to permit several processes to share access to the processor) multiprocessor systems really do involve genuinely concurrent processing, i.e. multiple processes are executing at exactly the same time (on different processors.)

When multiple processes are active at the same time, it is common that some of them will need to interact (one process providing information needed by another, one process determining the state of another, …). The interaction and synchronization of concurrent processes can become extremely subtle and complex Concurrency also creates the possibility of deadlock and/or starvation (as mentioned earlier, in chapter 2.)

4.1 Process Interaction/Synchronization

The way that concurrent processes communicate with each other is typically by leaving data/messages in commonly accessible memory locations (buffers.)

When concurrent processes can access common memory, however, many things can go wrong. "Synchronization" is a very complex issue and is subject to very subtle errors that can be extremely difficult to debug.

Nevertheless, synchronization is essential for concurrency to work.

4.1.1 Simple Producer-Consumer (Reader-Writer)

Consider a situation in which there are two processes, Prd and Cns, and each can access the same buffer Buf. Process Prd produces values and stores them in Buf to be used by Cns. Process Cns reads values from Buf and uses them for something (think of Cns as a printer driver and Prd as a process in a word processing program which stores text characters in Buf, for process Cns to send to a printer.)

Cns should not try to read a value from Buf until after Prd has placed a value there, and Prd should never try to store a new value in Buf until after Cns has removed any previous values. (We assume there can be only one instance of each procedure.)

One might be tempted to deal with this situation using the following combination of procedures:

```
procedure Prd(parVal)
    if ( Buf<>null ) pauseProcedure(Prd)
    Buf = parVal
    startProcedure( Cns )
    endProcedure(Prd)

procedure Cns()
    useValue(Buf)
    Buf=null
    if pausedProcedure ( Prd ) resumeProcedure( Prd )
    endProcedure(Cns)
```

The above pair of procedures DOES look like it should work.

When the main program starts, buffer Buf would initially contain null.
Some external process would provide a value for the parameter *parVal* and initiates execution of procedure Prd(*parVal*).
Since Buf contaims null, Prd does not pause, and *parVal* is stored in Buf.
Procedure Cns begins to execute and procedure Prd terminates.
Procedure Cns might complete (process the value in Buf, set Buf to null and, if procedure Prd is not in a paused state, Cns terminates) and nothing more happens until Prd is executed again.

It *might*, however, be the case that Prd might be reinitiated before Cns completes its action.

a) Possibly procedure Cns has not yet set Buf to null at the time that procedure Prd evaluates the expression (Buf<>null). In this case, procedure Prd will pause, procedure Cns will continue. It will set Buf to null, and, since Prd is paused, Cns will resume Prd. and terminate. (Note that, since only one instance of Cns is allowed, Prd cannot execute startProcedure(Cns) until Cns has terminated.)

b) If procedure Cns were to have executed (Buf=null) when Prd cones to have evaluated (Buf<>null) then Prd would not pause. It will store its new parameter value in Buf and attempt to execute startProcedure(Cns) Meanwhile Cns will not execute resumeProcedure(Prd). but instead simply terminate and at this point, Prd will be able to execute startProcedure(Cns) and will, terminate, and do nothing more until such time as the external process provides a new parVal and restarts procedure Prd.

c) The PROBLEM with the above construct is that (assuming, of course, that Prd and Cns are concurrent) the following scenario might conceivably occur:

1. Prd evaluates (Buf<>null) before Cns sets Buf to null

2. Before Prd can execute pauseProcedure(Prd), Cns continues, sets Buf to null, and then

3. , since Prd is Since pausedProcedure(Prd) is not true,Cns does not execute resumeProcedure(Prd) but simply continues on to its termination, endProcedure(Cns)

4. Now Prd executes pauseProcedure(Prd)

5. This leaves the system deadlocked, with a paused Prd and a nonexecuting Cns. Cns can only be restarted by Prd, but the paused Prd can only be resumed by Cns.

External process		Prd	Cns	Buf
		inactive	inactive	null
Prd(v1)		active	inactive	null
	Prd:(Buf<>null) is false	active	inactive	null
	Prd:(Buf=v1)	active	inactive	v1
	Prd:(startProcedure(Cns))	active	active	v1
	Prd:(endProcedure(Prd))	inactive	active	v1
Prd(v2)		active	active	v1
	Prd:(Buf<>null) is true	active	active	v1
	Cns:(useValue(Buf))	active	active	v1
	Cns:(Buf=null)	active	active	null
	Cns:(Prd not paused)	active	active	null
	Cns:(endProcedure(Cns))	active	inactive	null
	Prd:(pauseProcedure(Prd))	paused	inactive	null
Sequence leading to deadlocked Producer-Consumer 4.1.1				

4.1.2 Critical Regions

The example in 4.1.1 is typical of many synchronization situations. One way to avoid this kind of problem, is to ensure that any nontrivial process, once initiated, must be allowed to complete, before others can be allowed to continue.

In the case of 4.1.1 the process that must complete is
if (B<>null) pauseProcedure(P)

The common element of all (successful) synchronization schemes is a ***critical region*** whose execution must be handled as a unit without being interleaved with the execution of others.

Several mechanisms have been developed to implement critical regions. Among the most common are:

test-and-set: Test-and-set was first introduced by IBM for its 360/370 computers. The **test-and-set** instruction is an instruction used to write 1 (set) to a memory location and return its old value as a single atomic (i.e., non-interruptible) operation. If multiple processes may access the same memory location, and if a process is currently performing a test-and-set, no other process may begin another test-and-set until the first process's test-and-set is finished

semaphores: A semaphore is a nonnegative integer variable used as a flag. The variable, together with two uninterruptible unary operators, (traditionally identified as *P*, to test and decrement the value in the variable, and *V*, to increment the value in the variable[12]) form an abstract data type that is often used for access control to common resources used by multiple processes in concurrent systems.

The semaphore concept was invented by Dutch computer scientist Edsger Dijkstra in 1962 or 1963.

---

[12] The letters P and V are from the Dutch *proberen* (to test) and *verhogen* (to increment. The original designer of semaphores was Dutch, after all.

There are two types of semaphores, counting semaphores and binary semaphores.

4.1.2.1 Binary Semaphores

For a binary semaphore, the variable is restricted to the values 0 and 1. Binary semaphores are typically used to create/implement mutually exclusive critical regions (mutexes)

If S is a binary semaphore and a process attempts to execute P(S)

If the value of S is 1, then S is set to 0 and the process is allowed to continue (note that the operation P is atomic/uninterruptible, so no process can intervene between the testing of S being 1 or 0 and the modification of its value.)

If the value of S is 0, then the process is not allowed to proceed, but will be required to try executing P(S) again. The process might just be returned to the ready queue to wait for another turn, but more often it will be placed in the blocked queue, to be returned to the ready queue when the value of S changes to 1)

If S is a binary semaphore and a process executes V(S)

The value of S will be set to 1.

If S has an associated queue of blocked processes and this queue is not empty, one of the processes will be removed and returned to the ready queue, so that it can once again attempt to execute P(S)

4.1.2.2 Counting Semaphores

For a counting semaphore, the variable can take any nonnegative integer value. Counting semaphores are often used to keep track of the number of units of some type of resource in a system available for allocation.

If S is a counting semaphore and a process attempts to execute P(S)

If the value of S is 0, then, just as with binary semaphores, the process is not allowed to proceed, but will be required to try executing P(S) again. The process might just be returned to the ready queue to wait for another turn, but more often it will be placed in the blocked queue, to be returned to the ready queue when the value of S becomes nonnegative)

If the value of S is greater than 0, then the value of S will be decremented, and the process will be allowed to continue (note that the operation P is atomic/uninterruptible, so no process can intervene between the testing of S being 0 and the modification of its value.)

If S is a counting semaphore and a process executes V(S), the value in S will be incremented, and, if S has a nonempty queue of blocked processes they will be removed and reassigned to the ready queue so they can attempt to execute P(S) again.

4.1.2.3   Wait and Signal

The P and V operators are often described in terms of wait and signal actions

- **wait**: If the value of semaphore variable is positive, decrement it by 1 and continue. If the semaphore variable was 0, the process executing wait (P) is blocked, not allowed to proceed (required to *wait*) until the semaphore's value has become positive.

- **signal**: Increments the value of semaphore variable by 1 (or just sets it to 1 in case of a binary semaphore.) If the semaphore has any blocked processes, allow one of them to attempt to execute the wait operation again (*signal* the system that another resource has become available.)

4.1.2.1   Producer-Consumer (Reader-Writer) using Semaphores

Consider, again, the situation with two processes, Prd and Cns, and each can access the same buffer Buf. Process Prd produces values and stores them in Buf to be used by Cns. Process Cns reads values from Buf and *uses/consumes* them (in some way that we don't have to be really specific about.).

Cns should not try to read a value from Buf until after Prd has placed a value there, and Prd should not try to store a new value in Buf until after Cns has removed any previous values. In this example, we will use two semaphores (*writer*, initialized to 1, and *reader*, initialized to 0.)

We can deal with the producer-consumer situation (described above) using the following combination of procedures:

```
procedure Prd(parVal)
    P(writer)
    Buf = parVal
    startProcedure(Cns)
    V(reader)
    endProcedure(Prd)
```

```
procedure Cns()
    P(reader)
    useValue(Buf)
    V(writer)
    endProcedure(Cns).
```

With the above pair, when the external process provides a value *Parval* and executes Prd(*Parval*). The semaphore procedure P(writer) sets writer to 0, so any further attempts to execute W will be blocked until V(writer) is executed. Next Prd executes Buf=*Parval*, and then startProcedure(Cns). The first command in Cns is P(reader), but reader was initialized to 0, so Cns can proceed no further until V(reader) has been executed.

We don't want Cns to procced until procedure Prd has stored a value in Buf. Only after it does so, will Prd execute V(*reader*). At this point, further attempts by processes to execute Prd will be blocked by semaphore *writer* and will remain blocked until after Cns has processed the value in B and executed V(writer)

The sequence Prd:P(writer) … Prd: startProcedure(Cns) … Cns:V(writer) establishes a critical region in which no new instance of procedure Prd can begin executing

Similarly, (although probably of less importance for this situation) the sequence Cns:P(reader) … Prd:V(reader) establishes another critical region, this one making sure that only one instance of Cns can be active at any time.

4.1.3   More complex Producer-Consumer

Consider, now a more complex system. A system instead of having just one buffer to store a value, a system might have a number of resources that can be assigned/allocated to processes and deallocated as the process finish with them. (as an example, the various memory pages of RAM in a paging memory system.) The system might very well involve multiple processes (in a multiprogramming system) and each process might well be allocated multiple resources.

For this kind of situation, we can begin by representing the resources by entries in an array *resourceArray[ ]*, each entry of which is associated with a specific resource. The values of the entries in *resourceArray* will also have a field of type processID, and the values of these fields will all be initially be set to *null* (i.e. no process assigned.)

We will use three semaphores, two counting semaphores *Allocated* (initialized to 0) and *Available* (initialized to *Max*, the number of entries in the array, and the number of resources the system has) and one binary semaphore *Mutex*[13] (initialized to 1).

In our system, we will make use of two functions, *assign()* and *release()*

```
function assign(processID)
    P(Available)
    P(Mutex)
        i=0
        while (resourceArray[i].process<>null)
            i++
        resourceArray[i].process = processID
    V(Mutex)
return(resourceArray[i].resource)

procedure release(resourceID)
    P(Mutex)
        i=0
        while (resourceArray[i].resource<>resourceID)
            i++
        resourceArray[i].process = null
    V(Mutex)
    V(Available
```

With this construct, any number of simultaneous processes can attempt to execute function *assign()*. Each attempt will come to P(*Available*) and, if semaphore *Available* is 0, will be blocked, and placed in the semaphore's queue of blocked processes.

Because of our the initial settings, as many as *Max* processes might successfully execute P(*Available*) and attempt their next command P(*Mutex*). Mutex was initialized at 1, so when the first of the processes executes P(*Mutex*) the semaphore value becomes 0 and all other attempts will be placed in the *Mutex* waiting list. No further instance of *assign()* can execute P(*Mutex*) (nor can nor any instance of *release()* either for that matter) until that first instance of *assign()* has found an unassigned resource and assigned it to its process. After assign executes V(*Mutex*) which will return the value of the semaphore to 1 and release any processes from its waiting list, so that one of them might succeed in executing P(*Mutex*) and proceed in its path of execution.

---

[13] Mutex is a name tradionally assigned to a semaphore used for mutual exclusion. MUtual EXclusion

Any process, after having been assigned a resource, can later release it, executing the procedure *release*(resourceID), which will make that resource available for reassignment (setting the process field of its *resourceArray[ ]* entry to null) and increasing the count of available resources by executing V(*Available*)

4.2 Deadlock Prevention and Recovery

A deadlock occurs when there are several processes which have resources assigned, but cannot proceed because they need other resources which have been assigned to other processes, which also cannot proceed because they, in turn need resources which ... and so on.

Preventing/avoiding deadlocks requires that all processes identify all resources they will need before they are allowed to begin running. Any process which requires a resource already committed to an active process would have to wait (with no resources allocated) until processes using required resources have released them, and only then being released into the waiting queue for eventual execution. In early days of computing, when operating systems were batch systems, it was generally possible for programmers to identify all resources that would be needed by a program. With the advent of interactive systems, however, it has not been feasible to require users to identify in advance the resources that they will be using. For one thing, many interactive users are relatively unsophisticated and not keenly aware of exactly what resources their programs are using.

Interactive systems generally improve the use of resources through dynamic resource sharing, but dynamic resource sharing increases the chance of deadlocks.

When a deadlock occurs, the only way to recover, is to require a process to release one of the resources involved, so that another process can proceed. This, of course, might result in loss of information on the part of the process releasing the resource. In many general purpose systems such data loss can be tolerated, but in many others (especially many real time systems) such data loss could prove disastrous (systems such as hospital life support systems, aircraft guidance systems, …)

4.2.1   A deadlock situation can arise in a system if and only if all of the following conditions hold simultaneously in the system[14]:

1. *Mutual exclusion:* At least one resource must be held in a non-shareable mode. Otherwise, the processes would not be prevented from using the resource when necessary.

2. *Hold and wait* or *resource holding:* a process is currently holding at least one resource and requesting additional resources which are being held by other processes.

3. *No preemption:* a resource can be released only voluntarily by the process holding it.

4. *Circular wait:* each process must be waiting for a resource which is being held by another process, which in turn is waiting for the first process to release the resource. In general, there is a set of waiting processes, $\{P_1, P_2, \ldots, P_N\}$, such that P_1 is waiting for a resource held by P_2, P_2 is waiting for a resource held by P_3 and so on until P_N is waiting for a resource held by P_1.

Most current operating systems cannot prevent deadlocks. When a deadlock occurs, different operating systems respond to them in different manners. Most of the approaches work by preventing one of the four Coffman conditions from occurring (most commonly the circular wait condition.)

Major approaches are as follows.

a. *Ignoring deadlock:*In this approach, it is assumed that a deadlock will never occur. This approach was initially used by MINIX and UNIX. This would be appropriate when the time intervals between occurrences of deadlocks are large and the data loss incurred each time is tolerable. In this case, when deadlocks DO occur, human/operator intervention is required (most likely a system reboot.)

b. *Detection*: Under the deadlock detection, deadlocks are allowed to occur. Then the state of the system is examined to detect that a deadlock has occurred and subsequently it is corrected. An algorithm is employed that tracks resource allocation and process states, it rolls back and restarts one or more of the processes in order to remove the detected deadlock. Detecting a deadlock that has already occurred is easily possible since the resources that

---

[14]   These four conditions are known as the *Coffman conditions* from their first description in a 1971 article by Edward G. Coffman, Jr.

each process has locked and/or currently requested are known to the resource scheduler of the operating system. After a deadlock is detected, it can be corrected by using one of the following methods:

i.   *Process termination:* one or more processes involved in the deadlock may be aborted.

   1. One could choose to abort all competing processes involved in the deadlock. This ensures that deadlock is resolved with certainty and speed, but the expense is high since partial computations will be lost.

   2. One could choose to abort one process at a time until the deadlock is resolved. This approach has high overhead because after each abort an algorithm must determine whether the system is still in deadlock. In this case, several factors should be considered while choosing a candidate for termination; factors such as such as priorities and ages of the processes.]

ii. *Resource preemption:* resources allocated to various processes may be successively preempted and allocated to other processes until the deadlock is broken.

c.   Prevention: Deadlock prevention works by preventing one of the four Coffman conditions from occurring.

   i.   Removing the *mutual exclusion* condition means that no process will have exclusive access to a resource. Algorithms that avoid mutual exclusion are called **non-blocking** synchronization algorithms.

   ii. The *hold and wait* or *resource holding* conditions may be removed by requiring processes to request all the resources they will need before starting up (or before embarking upon a particular set of operations). This advance knowledge is frequently difficult to satisfy and, in any case, is an inefficient use of resources. Another way is to require that a process request resources only when it has none. Thus, first they must release all their currently held resources before requesting all the resources they will need from scratch. This too is often impractical. It is impractical because resources may be allocated and remain unused for long periods. Also, a process requiring a popular resource may have to wait indefinitely, as such a resource may always be allocated to some other process, resulting in resource starvation. (These algorithms are known as the **all-or-none** *algorithms*.)

   iii. The *no preemption* condition may also be difficult or impossible to avoid as a process has to be able to have a resource for a certain amount of time, or the processing outcome may be inconsistent, or thrashing may occur. However, inability to enforce preemption may interfere with a *priority* algorithm. Preemption of a "locked out" resource generally implies a rollback, and is to be avoided, since it is very costly in overhead. Algorithms that allow preemption include *lock-free* and **wait-free** algorithms and ***optimistic concurrency control***. If a process is holding some resources and requests some additional resource(s) that cannot be immediately allocated to it, the condition may be removed by releasing all the currently being held resources of that process.

iv.   The final condition is the *circular wait* condition. Approaches that avoid circular waits include disabling interrupts during critical sections and using a hierarchy to determine a partial ordering of resources. If no obvious hierarchy exists, even the memory address of resources has been used to determine ordering and resources are requested in the increasing order of the enumeration.

4.3   Process Starvation

Starvation is the name given to indefinite postponement of process because it requires some resources before it can run but the resource(s) is/are never allocated to this process, usually because the necessary resource(s) is/are widely used, and the system tends to have numerous higher priority processes making use of it/them.

A common technique to avoid starvation is *aging*, i.e. periodically increasing the priorities of processes that have been blocked for long periods of time. This way, a process that has frequently been denied access to a resource will eventually have its priority raised above that of its competitors and be granted access to the resource.

4.4 Exercises:

4.4.1   In 4.1.2.1   Binary Semaphores, when executing V(S) and the value in S is 0, it is quite possible that there will be multiple processes in the queue of blocked processes. Should all be removed to the ready queue, or only one? What would be the consequences of removing one process and of removing all?

4.4.2   In 4.1.2.2   Counting Semaphores, when executing V(S), it is quite possible that there will be multiple processes in the queue of blocked processes. Should all of them be removed to the ready queue, or only one? What would be the consequences of removing one process and of removing all?

4.4.3   In the structure of 4.1.3, analyze the consequences of changing the sequences

a) in function *release*(), placing P(*Available*) immediately after P(*Mutex*) rather than immediately before.

b) in function *release*(), placing return(resourceArray[i].resource) before V(Mutex) rather than after.

c) in procedure release(), placing V(Available) immediately before V(Mutex) instead of immediately after.

4.4.4   In setting up the structure of 4.1.3, we assumed that all resources are constant, all either assigned to processes or available for assignment. In a situation such as an airline reservation system, however, resources would be removed from the system (a flight leaves, so no new reservations can be accepted for its seats) and new resources introduced into the system (new flights have their seats made available for booking.). In such a system, then, in addition to assign() and release(), we would also need an addResource() process and removeResource() process. Describe the variables, semaphores and processes to implement such a system

4.5 Chapter 4 Questions

4.5.1   True-False

4.5.1.1   All modern operating systems have to deal with the problems of concurrent processes (processes dealing with things that are going on simultaneously.)

4.5.1.2   When concurrent processes can access common memory, many things can go wrong.

4.5.1.3   There is a unique mechanism which has been developed to implement critical regions.

4.5.1.4 In early days of computing, when operating systems were batch systems, it was generally possible for programmers to identify all resources that would be needed by a program. With the advent of interactive systems, however, it has not been feasible to require users to identify in advance the resources that they will be using

4.5.1.5 Dynamic resource sharing tends to decrease the chance of deadlocks.

4.5.1.6 Detecting a deadlock that has already occurred is easily possible

4.5.1.7 Most current operating systems cannot prevent deadlocks

4.5.2 Multiple Choice

4.5.2.1 The common element of all (successful) synchronization schemes is that of a _____ whose execution must be handled as a unit without being interleaved with the execution of others.
a. *critical region*
b. *hot area*
c. *singular section*
d. *controlling process*
e. none of the above

4.5.2.2 *semaphores:* one of the mechanisms developed to implement critical regions, were invented by _____
a. Brinch-Hansen
b. Deitel
c. Hamming
d. Tannenbaum
e. none of the above

4.5.3 Completion

4.5.3.1 All modern operating systems have to deal with the problems of _____ processes (processes dealing with things that are going on simultaneously.)

4.5.3.2 When multiple processes are active at the same time, it is common that some of them will need to _____

4.5.3.3 Concurrency creates the possibility of _____ and/or starvation

4.5.3.4 The way that concurrent processes communicate with each other is typically by leaving data/messages in commonly accessible memory locations (_____.)

4.5.3.5 The _____ instruction is an instruction used to write 1 to a memory location and return its old value as a single **atomic** (i.e., non-interruptible) operation

4.5.3.6 _____ semaphores are typically used to create/implement mutually exclusive critical regions

4.5.3.7 _____ is a name tradionally assigned to a semaphore used for mutual exclusion

4.5.3.8 **Preventing deadlock by** removing the *mutual exclusion* condition means that no process will have exclusive access to a resource. Algorithms that avoid mutual exclusion are called _____ synchronization algorithms

4.5.3.9 _____ is the name given to indefinite postponement of process because it requires some resources before it can run but the resource(s) is/are never allocated to this process, usually because the necessary resource(s) is/are widely used, and the system tends to have numerous higher priority processes making use of it/them.

5. Policies for Assigning Processor Time

Although most modern computing systems have several processors, the operating systems will typically deal with situations involving more jobs/processes than there are processors, so there will be a number of processes waiting to use a processor and there must be some system/policy for choosing a process when a processor becomes available. There are a number of different policies that have been used, and the policy chosen for a given system will usually depend on what kind of system it is and what it is used for[15].

Policies for processor selection can be divided into two classes: Preemptive and Non-Preemptive.

> In a *non-preemptive* system, a process, once it is given access to a processor, will be allowed to continue using that processor until it relinquishes control (having finished its task, having come to a point where it needs the results of some I/O operation, or must pause for some other reason.) When the process relinquishes control, the operating system assigns the processor to another process.

> In a *preemptive* system, processes are given access to a processor for a fixed (maximum) period of time (a *time slice* aka *quantum*) The process might well relinquish control before the time slice ends, but if it does not, it will be interrupted. In either case, another process will then be allowed to use the processor.

Very few modern systems are non-preemptive, almost all are preemptive. Systems will differ primarily on length of time slices and priorities for processes in the waiting queue.

Some systems might be designed to prioritize:

> *throughput* (maximize the number of jobs that can be completed)

> *response time* (minimize the time that each user must wait for response)

> *cpu efficiency* (maximize the proportion of time that processor is executing process code[16])

> *job fairness* (each job gets same execution time)

> *system capacity* (maximize number of simultaneous processes/users that the system can/will support)

---

[15] The policies on a personal computer will be very different from those of a large time sharing system, and those will be different from those used on a supercomputer.

[16] **Note:** CPU utilization on a device should never reach 100 percent because a device running at 100 percent CPU utilization might be slow to respond to management or system events.

Systems can also be (and usually are) designed to enforce (other) externally assigned priorities. These priorities will, of course, vary from one system to another, depending on the function of the system, and most systems will involve a combination of the above and will normally be designed to avoid deadlocks and starvation. A priority system aimed at only one of the above would be simplistic and create problems:

A system prioritizing *throughput* would give highest priority to the shortest jobs and might use relatively long time slices to avoid the overhead involved in unnecessary switching from one process to another. This, however, creates the danger of longer jobs suffering process starvation.

To minimize *response time* a system would prioritize I/O bound (interactive) processes, and use short time slices to maximize the number of processes working toward the point where they need user interaction. Compute bound processes would obviously suffer from this system.

To maximize *cpu efficiency* a system would use long time slices and prioritize compute bound processes to minimize the frequency of process switching. In such a system response time might suffer and I/O bound processes could conceivably suffer starvation.

A system prioritizing *fairness* would use a simple fifo waiting queue and assign no process priorities. In a busy system with numerous compute bound processes, such a system might result in poor response time.

A system prioritizing *capacity* would prioritize small/short I/O bound processes. Small processes would occupy less RAM, and so more would fit into memory. I/O bound processes spend more time in a paused state, and so put less burden on the processor(s). Larger compute bound processes might suffer starvation.

5.1   Processor Scheduling Algorithms

There are a number of algorithms used by systems for CPU allocation. Some of these algorithms are:

FCFS/FIFO   (First Come First Served/First In First Out) is the simplest scheduling algorithm. It simply queues processes in the order that they arrive. Usually implemented as a non-preemptive system. Once a process has the CPU, it runs to completion. Overhead is minimal. Assuming all processes complete, there would be no starvation. As non-preemptive system, it is only suitable for batch processing, and, as such, was only used on earliest batch processing systems.

EDF   (Earliest Deadline First) Processes are placed in a queue ordered by deadlines by which they should complete. (A form of priority scheduling.) This algorithm is not widely used in a pure form, since behavior is problematic in systems that could become overloaded. Deadline time has the effect of aging, so starvation would not be a problem, as long as system never overloads.

SJN/SJF   (Shortest Job Next, Shortest Job First) Waiting processes are kept in a queue ordered by (estimated) time required to complete execution. When a processor becomes available, the process with shortest execution time is chosen. SJN is a non-preemptive algorithm. The shortest job retains the CPU until it completes (or interrupts.) SRT (below) is a preemptive variant of SJN. Shortest job next has advantages of simplicity. It tends to maximize throughput and minimize (average) response time (defined as the average amount of time each process has to wait until its execution begins.) It does, however, have the potential for process starvation. If short processes are continually added, longer processes might never get to run. Again, pure SJN is only suitable for batch systems. It is non-preemptive and requires an estimate of execution time, which is generally not available for interactive processes.

HRRN   (Highest response ratio next) HRRN scheduling is another non-preemptive discipline. It was developed by Brinch Hansen as modification of SJN to mitigate the problem of process starvation. In HRRN, the next job is not that with the shorted estimated run time, but that with the highest response ratio defined as

responseRatio=(timeWaiting+estimatedRunTime)/estimatedRunTime

This means, the jobs that have spent a long time waiting compete against those estimated to have short run times.

HRRN is a form of priority scheduling (PS) which is designed to implement *aging*.

SRT   (Shortest Remaining Time) Similar to shortest job first. With this strategy the scheduler arranges processes with the least estimated processing time remaining to be next in the queue. This requires advanced knowledge (or estimates of) the time required for a process to complete. If a shorter process arrives during another process' execution, the currently running process is interrupted, and its estimated time to complete must be updated, before returning the interrupted process to the waiting queue. This, of course, adds to the system overhead. The scheduler must also place each incoming process into a specific place in the queue, creating additional overhead. The SRT algorithm is designed for maximum throughput in most scenarios, but because of increased overhead, might, in fact, be slower than SJN. Waiting time and response time increase as the process's computational requirements increase. Since turnaround time is based on waiting time plus processing time, longer processes are significantly affected by this.

Starvation is possible, especially in a busy system with many small processes being run.

RR   (Round Robin[xv]) RR is a preemptive scheduling system. The scheduler assigns a fixed time unit per process, and cycles through them. If process completes within that time-slice it gets terminated otherwise it is rescheduled after giving a chance to all other processes. RR scheduling involves considerable overhead (especially with a small time unit.) It results in throughput between that of FCFS and SJF. Shorter jobs are completed faster than in FCFS and longer processes are completed faster than in SJF. It generally has good average response time, since waiting times depend on number of processes, and not lengths of other processes. Starvation will never occur, since no priority is given.

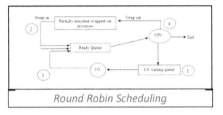

Round Robin Scheduling

PS   (Priority Scheduling) Non-preemptive priority scheduling is one of the most common scheduling systems in batch systems. It gives preferential treatment to some jobs at the cost of other less important ones. (SJF is an example of PS scheduling.) The programs with highest priorities are processed first and are not interrupted until they complete or pause themselves.

Priorities can be assigned based on many different characteristics (who the user is, how much memory required, what peripheral devices required, total run time, how long it has been waiting (i.e. *aging*), and many others.)

FPPS   Fixed-priority preemptive scheduling is a scheduling system commonly used in real-time systems. With fixed priority preemptive scheduling, the scheduler ensures that at any given time, the processor executes the highest priority task of all those tasks that are currently ready to execute. The process is given a time slice (quantum) and, when the process self-interrupts, or completes, or finishes its time slice, the preemptive scheduler has the option of once again identifying the highest priority task from among those ready to execute. This scheduling system has the advantage of making sure no task hogs the processor for any time longer than the time slice. However, this scheduling scheme is vulnerable to process or thread lockout: since priority is given to higher-priority tasks, the lower-priority tasks could wait an indefinite amount of time. One common method of arbitrating this situation is aging, which gradually increments the priority of waiting processes and threads, ensuring that they will all eventually execute. Most real-time operating systems (RTOS's) have preemptive schedulers.

CFS (Completely Fair Scheduler) is a process scheduler which was merged into the 2.6.23 (October 2007) release of the Linux kernel[xvi] and is the default scheduler. It handles CPU resource allocation for executing processes and aims to maximize overall CPU utilization while also maximizing interactive performance.

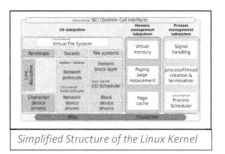
Simplified Structure of the Linux Kernel

Like the old O(1) scheduler, CFS uses a concept called "sleeper fairness", which considers sleeping or waiting tasks equivalent to those on the runqueue. This means that interactive tasks which spend most of their time waiting for user input or other events get a comparable share of CPU time when they need it.

Multiple Level Queues[xvii] When processes can be readily categorized, then multiple separate queues can be established, each implementing whatever scheduling algorithm is most appropriate for that type of job, and/or with different parametric adjustments.

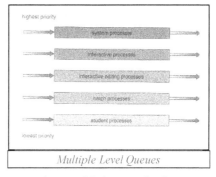
Multiple Level Queues

This type of system is used for situations in which processes can be divided into different groups. (One example could be made between foreground/interactive processes and background/batch processes. These two types of processes have different response-time requirements and so may have different scheduling needs. Another common subdivision is that of I/O bound and compute bound processes.)

Scheduling must also be done between queues, that is scheduling one queue to get time relative to other queues. Two common options are:

strict priority (no job in a lower priority queue runs until all higher priority queues are empty)

and *round-robin* (each queue gets a time slice in turn. (Some systems assign different time slice sizes for processes from different queues.)

Note that under this algorithm jobs cannot switch from queue to queue - Once they are assigned a queue, that is their queue until they finish.

Multilevel Feedback-Queue Scheduling[xviii]
scheduling is similar to the ordinary
multilevel queue scheduling described
above, except that jobs may be moved
from one queue to another for a variety
of reasons:

Multilevel feedback queue

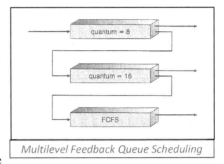

Multilevel Feedback Queue Scheduling

o   If the characteristics of a job
     change between CPU-intensive and
     I/O intensive, then it may be
     appropriate to switch a job from one
     queue to another.

o   Aging can also be incorporated, so that a job that has waited for a long
     time can get bumped up into a higher priority queue for a while.

Multilevel feedback queue scheduling is the more flexible, because it can be
tuned for any situation. But it is also much more complex to implement
because of all the adjustable parameters.

Some of the parameters which define one of these systems include:

o   The number of queues.

o   The scheduling algorithm for each queue.

o   The methods used to upgrade or demote processes from one queue to
     another. (Which may not be the same for all queues)

o   The method used to determine which queue a process enters initially.

5.2 Processor Affinity[xix]

When designing a scheduling algorithm for a multiprocessor system, there is the
additional problem of identifying which processor to use for a given process. Should
some of the processes have "preferred" processors, or should a process, when its
turn comes in the waiting queue, simply be assigned to the first processor that comes
available.

One of the important factors in this decision is cache memory. Processors contain
cache memory which speeds up repeated accesses to the same memory locations. If
a process were to switch from one processor to another each time it got a time slice,
the data in the cache (for that process) would have to be invalidated and re-loaded
from main memory, and this would eliminate the benefit of the cache.

Usually then, systems attempt to keep assigning processes to the same processor, via
processor affinity.

Soft affinity occurs when the system attempts to keep processes on the same processor but makes no guarantees.

Hard affinity, on the other hand, describes a system in which a process specifies that it is not to be moved between processors. Linux (as well as some other OSes) support ***hard affinity***.

Main memory architecture can also affect process affinity, if particular CPUs have faster access to memory on the same chip or board than to other memory loaded elsewhere. (Non-Uniform Memory Access, NUMA.) If a process has an affinity for a particular CPU, then it should preferentially be assigned memory storage in "local" fast access areas.

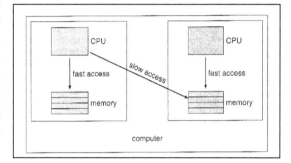

5.2.1 Virtualization and Scheduling

Virtualization adds another layer of complexity and scheduling. Typically, there is one host operating system operating on "real" processor(s) and a number of guest operating systems operating on virtual processors. The Host OS creates some number of virtual processors and presents them to the guest OSes as if they were real processors. The guest OSes don't realize their processors are virtual and make scheduling decisions on the assumption that they are real processors. As a result, interactive and especially real-time performance can be severely compromised on guest systems.

5.3 Questions

5.3.1 True-False

5.3.1.1 Since most modern computing systems have several processors, it is rare for the operating systems to have to deal with situations involving more jobs/processes than there are processors

5.3.1.2 Very few modern systems are non-preemptive, almost all are preemptive

5.3.1.3 A device running at 100 percent CPU utilization would be very quick to respond to management or system events.

5.3.1.4 One of the primary advantages of RR scheduling is that it involves relatively little overhead

5.3.2 Multiple Choice

5.3.2.1 To _____ a system would prioritize I/O bound (interactive) processes, and use short time slices to maximize the number of processes working toward the point where they need user interaction. Compute bound processes would obviously suffer from this system
a.   minimize *response time*
b.   maximize *cpu efficiency*
c.   prioritize *fairness*
d.   prioritize *capacity*
e.   none of the above

5.3.2.2 To _____ a system would use a simple fifo waiting queue and assign no process priorities.
a.   minimize *response time*
b.   maximize *cpu efficiency*
c.   prioritize *fairness*
d.   prioritize *capacity*
e.   none of the above

5.3.2.3 There are a number of algorithms used by systems for CPU allocation. One of these _____ is the simplest, but was only used on the earlieest batch processing systems
a.   FIFO
b.   SJF
c.   HRRN
d.   FPPS
e.   none of the above

5.3.2.4   There are a number of algorithms used by systems for CPU allocation. One of these _____ is the default scheduler for the Linux kernel
   a.   FIFO
   b.   SJF
   c.   HRRN
   d.   FPPS
   e.   none of the above

5.3.2.5   There are a number of algorithms used by systems for CPU allocation. One of these _____ places processes in a queue ordered by estimated processing time remaining
   a.   EDF
   b.   SRT
   c.   RR
   d.   PS
   e.   none of the above

5.3.3   Completion

5.3.3.1   In a(n) _____ system, a process, once it is given access to a processor, will be allowed to continue using that processor until it relinquishes control

5.3.3.2   A system is said to prioritize _____ if it is designed to maximize the number of jobs that can be completed

5.3.3.3   PS is one of the most common scheduling systems in _____ systems.

5.3.3.4   _____ *affinity* occurs when the system attempts to keep processes on the same processor but makes no guarantees

6. Memory Management

Recall (from chapter 1) external storage is much cheaper than RAM, so it seems obvious that a larger number of processes can be accommodated (on a system of the same price) if suspended programs would be stored on disk, rather than occupying relatively expensive RAM, (at least until they are ready to resume execution.) Systems can use disk space as an extension of their memory space (virtual memory systems.) The effectiveness of virtual memory systems can be attributed in large part to the "Principle of Locality"

6.1 Virtual Memory Systems

Virtual memory systems have been developed to identify sections of RAM that are unlikely to be referenced in the immediate future and to copy these sections to disk, allowing those areas of RAM to be used by other processes (or even sections of the same process that aren't currently in memory.) These sections of memory copied to disk might include entire programs that are paused waiting on I/O, but could also include subsections of a relatively large program even while that program executes. A large program might be divided into sections, and while it is executing, using commands and data in one section, other sections of the program might not be in use and could be swapped out to disk.

This, of course, adds to the complexity of the operating systems. Now they are also required to manage virtual memory systems: they must identify which programs and/or program segments will (probably) not be referenced immediately; they must keep track of where on disk the pages/segments are stored; they must be able to retrieve them; they must determine where in RAM to copy them after retrieval.

Virtual memory systems can be effective in large part because of the "Principle of Locality". This principle states that memory references by the processor tend to cluster. If, for a reasonable period of time, none of the cells in a particular section of memory have been referenced, then it is likely that the next several memory references will continue to be to cells in a different section of memory, and so, if the "*none reference*" section were to be swapped out, the system performance would not be affected (for a while.)

Disk access involves two steps: The movement of an arm to place a read/write head over the correct track (the time that it takes to do this is called the seek time for the access) and then the rotation of the disk to align the desired sector with the head the time that it takes to do this is called the *rotational latency* of the access.) Seek time is typically much longer than rotational latency. This means that data transfer to and from a disk is much more efficient if sections of data that will be referenced together are stored on the same disk track, or at least on tracks very close together and, hence, requiring little arm movement to read or write related information. This provided the motivation for the development of *paging* systems.

Virtual memory systems are subject to **thrashing**, which occurs when the computer's virtual memory resources become saturated, leading to a constant state of exchanging data in memory for data on disk, to the exclusion of most application-level processing.

6.2   *Paging memory systems*:

As we have seen, it had become necessary to design a system that would support the efficient repositioning of programs and data, both between RAM and cache and between RAM and hard disk. The system that was developed is called *paging*.

The OS has five principal storage management responsibilities:
>   process isolation;
>   allocation and management;
>   modular programming support;
>   protection and access control
>   long-term storage,

and paging systems provide support for all of these.

Paging is a system in which processes are made up of a number of fixed size blocks, called pages. In a paging system, a program references a word by means of a *virtual address*, which is implemented as a *page number* and an *offset* within the page. Each page can be located anywhere in main memory. Paging provides a system for a dynamic mapping between the virtual addresses used in the program and real (or physical) addresses in main memory. Such a system is necessary to support a virtual memory system. In order to minimize access times, the contents of a page will normally be stored in the same disk sector or (less frequently) in adjacent disk sectors. Thus page sizes tend to be dictated by sector sizes on attached hard disks.

6.2.1   Virtual Memory Addressing[xx]

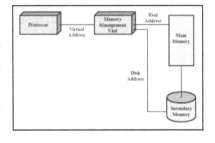

In a system using virtual memory (with paging) processes and data sets will be organized in files, each occupying one or more pages on secondary storage. (Some pages will have copies in primary storage, and some will not. The CPU, of course, can only deal directly with locations in primary storage.)

When a CPU references an entity in such a system, it identifies the page of the entity, and its location (offset) within the page. The Memory Management Unit will have a table of the pages, and records of whether they have copies in RAM (and, if so, where in RAM they are located.) When the processor references an address on a page, the Memory Management Unit determines whether that page is in RAM. If it is, the MMU directs the reference to the appropriate RAM address. If the page with the referenced location is not in RAM, the Memory management Unit pauses the CPU process and initiates the process of copying referenced page into RAM.

6.2.2 Virtual Memory with Paging[xxi]

When a process begins execution in a virtual memory system implemented by paging, only the page containing its initial section is called into memory. The principle of locality suggests that the first few operations will reference memory locations in that page. If, at some point, a location on another page is referenced, then the process will

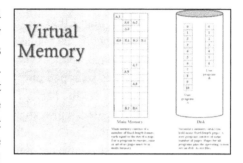

pause, the system will find, or create space in RAM for that page. When the new page has been loaded, the process can continue executing.

If there are many processes executing, it is likely that all available memory would be in use and, when a memory reference is made to a location not currently in RAM, there would be no unused RAM locations a new page. In such a case the contents of some RAM page must be copied to disk. Then the page with the referenced address can be copied from disk into the RAM whose contents were just saved. This system requires some policy for identifying which pages might be copied to disk. Often such a system involves an algorithm for predicting which pages would be unlikely be referenced in the immediate future. There are a number of possible strategies. Among them are:

FIFO (First In First Out) The page to be replaced would be the one that has been in RAM the longest. This strategy is relatively easy to implement, and it seems intuitive that a page that has been in RAM for the longest might be less likely to be referenced in the near future than others that were copied into RAM more recently. Unfortunately, in many systems this algorithm has been seen to target popular library functions used by many processes. Commonly used functions will tend to get referenced (and copied into RAM) early (and often.) When swapped out, these pages will be referenced, and copied back into RAM almost immediately. Although FIFO is a poor predictor of future inactivity, it is one of the simplest strategies to implement. It is a low-overhead algorithm that requires little bookkeeping on the part of the operating system. The idea is obvious from the name – the operating system keeps track of all the pages in memory in a queue, with the most recent arrival at the back, and the oldest arrival in front. When a page needs to be replaced, the page at the front of the queue (the oldest page) is selected. While FIFO is cheap and intuitive, it performs poorly in practical application. Thus, it is rarely used in its unmodified form. The FIFO page replacement algorithm is used by the VAX/VMS operating system, but with some modifications. Partial second chance (see below) is one of these modifications

Second-chance: A modified form of the FIFO page replacement algorithm, known as the *Second-chance* page replacement algorithm, fares relatively better than FIFO at little cost for the improvement. It works by looking at the front of the queue as FIFO does, but instead of immediately paging out that page, it checks to see if its *referenced bit*[17] is set. If it is not set, the page is swapped out. Otherwise, the referenced bit is cleared, the page is inserted at the back of the queue (as if it were a new page) and this process is repeated. This can also be thought of as a circular queue. If all the pages have their referenced bit set, on the second encounter of the first page in the list, that page will be swapped out, as it now has its referenced bit cleared. If all the pages have their reference bit cleared, then second chance algorithm degenerates into pure FIFO. As its name suggests, Second-chance gives every page a "second-chance" – an old page that has been referenced is probably in use and should not be swapped out instead of a new page that has not been referenced.

Clock is a more efficient version of FIFO than second-chance because pages don't have to be constantly pushed to the back of the list, but it performs the same general function as Second-Chance. The clock algorithm keeps a circular list of pages in memory, with the "hand" (iterator) pointing to the last examined page frame in the list. When a page fault occurs and no empty frames exist, then the R (referenced) bit is inspected at the hand's location. If R is 0, the new page is put in place of the page the "hand" points to. Otherwise, the R bit is cleared, then the clock hand is incremented and the process is repeated until a page is replaced.

LRU (Least Recently Used) This strategy replaces the page that has gone the longest without a reference. According to the principle of locality, this should give the best performance. Unfortunately, it is more difficult to implement efficiently. It tends to require more processing and storage overhead than do

---

[17] When a page is referenced, a *referenced bit* is set for that page, marking it as referenced. Similarly, when a page is modified (written to), a modified bit is set. The setting of the bits is usually done by the hardware, although it is possible to do so on the software level. At a certain fixed time interval, a timer interrupt triggers and clears the referenced bit of all the pages, so only pages referenced within the current timer interval are marked with a referenced bit.

other techniques. The least recently used (LRU) page replacement algorithm, though similar in name to NRU (described below), differs in the fact that LRU keeps track of page usage over a short period of time, while NRU just looks at the usage in the last clock interval. LRU works on the idea that pages that have been most heavily used in the past few instructions are most likely to be used heavily in the next few instructions too. While LRU can provide near-optimal performance in theory, it is rather expensive to implement in practice. There are a few implementation methods for this algorithm that try to reduce the cost yet keep as much of the performance as possible.

The most expensive method is the linked list method, which uses a linked list containing all the pages in memory. At the back of this list is the least recently used page, and at the front is the most recently used page. The cost of this implementation lies in the fact that items in the list will have to be moved with every memory reference, which is a very time-consuming process.

Another method that requires hardware support is as follows: suppose the hardware has a 64-bit counter that is incremented at every instruction. Whenever a page is accessed, it acquires the value equal to the counter at the time of page access. Whenever a page needs to be replaced, the operating system selects the page with the lowest counter and swaps it out. With present hardware, this is not feasible because the OS would need to examine the counter for every page in memory.

Because of implementation costs, one may consider algorithms that are similar to LRU, but which offer cheaper implementations. One important advantage of the LRU algorithm is that it is amenable to full statistical analysis. It has been proven, for example, that LRU can never result in more than N-times more page faults than the optimum algorithm, where N is proportional to the number of pages in the managed pool.

On the other hand, LRU's weakness is that its performance tends to degenerate under many quite common reference patterns.

For example, if there are N pages in the LRU pool, an application executing a loop over array of N + 1 pages will cause a page fault on each and every access. As loops over large arrays are common, much effort has been put into modifying LRU to work better in such situations. Many of the proposed LRU modifications try to detect looping reference patterns and to switch into a more suitable replacement algorithm, like Most Recently Used (MRU).

LFU (Least Frequently Used) This technique can be implemented more efficiently (with less overhead) than LRU, but has a tendency to target the most recently loaded pages before they have an opportunity to have established themselves as being used frequently.

NRU (Not Recently Used) The not recently used (NRU) page replacement algorithm is an algorithm that favors keeping pages in memory that have been recently used. This algorithm uses the following technique: when a page is referenced, a *referenced* bit is set for that page, marking it as having been referenced. Similarly, when a page is modified (written to), a *modified* bit is set. The setting of the bits is usually done by the hardware, although it is possible to do so on the software level as well. At a certain fixed time interval, a timer interrupt triggers and clears the referenced bit of all the pages, so only pages referenced within the current timer interval are marked with a referenced bit. When a page needs to be replaced, the operating system divides the pages into four classes:

3. referenced, modified

2. referenced, not modified

1. not referenced, modified

0. not referenced, not modified

Although it might not seem possible for a page to be modified yet not referenced, this happens when a class 3 page has its referenced bit cleared by the timer interrupt. The NRU algorithm picks a random page from the lowest category for removal. So out of the above four page categories, the NRU algorithm will replace a not-referenced, not-modified page if such a page exists. Note that this algorithm implies that a modified but not-referenced (within the last timer interval) page is less important than a not-modified page that is intensely referenced.

NFU (Not frequently used) The not frequently used page replacement algorithm requires a counter, and every page has one counter of its own which is initially set to 0. At each clock interval, all pages that have been referenced within that interval will have their counter incremented by 1. In effect, the counters keep track of how frequently a page has been used. Thus, the page with the lowest counter can be swapped out when necessary. The main problem with NFU is that it keeps track of the frequency of use without regard to the time span of use. Thus, in a multi-pass compiler, pages which were heavily used during the first pass, but are not needed in the second pass will be favored over pages which are comparably lightly used in the second pass, as they have higher frequency counters. This results in poor performance. Other common scenarios also exist where NFU will perform similarly One such is an OS boot-up.

Aging: The aging algorithm is a descendant of the NFU algorithm, with modifications to make it aware of the time span of use. Instead of just incrementing the counters of pages referenced, putting equal emphasis on page references regardless of the time, the reference counter on a page is first shifted right (divided by 2), before adding the referenced bit to the left of that binary number. For instance, if a page has referenced bits 1,0,0,1,1,0 in the past 6 clock ticks, its referenced counter will look like this: 10000000, 01000000, 00100000, 10010000, 11001000, 01100100. Page references closer to the current time have more impact than earlier page references. This ensures that pages referenced more recently, even though less frequently, will have higher priority over pages frequently referenced in the past. Of course, when a page needs to be swapped out, the page with the lowest counter will be chosen.

Random Although not widely used, the strategy of simply choosing a page at random actually works almost as well as most others and has the advantage of being easy to implement and with virtually no overhead. Random replacement algorithm replaces a random page in memory. This eliminates the overhead cost of tracking page references. Usually it fares better than FIFO, and for looping memory references it is better than LRU, although generally LRU performs better in practice. OS/390 uses global LRU approximation and falls back to random replacement when LRU performance degenerates, and the Intel i860 processor used a random replacement.

6.2.3 Developments Concerning Page Replacement Algorithms

Page replacement algorithms were a hot topic of research and debate in the 1960s and 1970s. That mostly ended with the development of sophisticated LRU (least recently used) approximations and working set algorithms. Since then, though, some basic assumptions made by the traditional page replacement algorithms were invalidated, resulting in a revival of research. In particular, the following trends in the behavior of underlying hardware and user-level software have affected the performance of page replacement algorithms:

Size of primary storage has increased by multiple orders of magnitude. With several gigabytes of primary memory, algorithms that require a periodic check of every memory frame are becoming less and less practical.

Locality of reference has weakened for user software. This is mostly attributed to the spread of object-oriented programming techniques that favor large numbers of small functions and the use of sophisticated data structures like trees and hash tables that tend to result in chaotic memory reference patterns.

In addition, requirements for page replacement algorithms have changed due to differences in operating system **kernel** architectures. In particular, most modern OS kernels have unified virtual memory and file system caches, requiring the page replacement algorithm to select a page from among the pages of both user program virtual address spaces and cached files. The latter pages have specific properties. For example, they can be locked, or can have write ordering requirements imposed. Moreover, as the goal of page replacement is to minimize total time waiting for memory, it has to take into account memory requirements imposed by other kernel sub-systems that allocate memory. As a result, page replacement in modern kernels (**Linux**, **FreeBSD**, and **Solaris**) tends to work at the level of a general purpose kernel memory allocator, rather than at the higher level of a virtual memory subsystem.

6.3   Memory Segmentation

Memory segmentation is the division of a computer's primary memory into **segments** or **sections**. Unlike pages, segments are not generally of uniform sizes, and are generally controlled by programmers, rather than the operating system.

In a computer system using segmentation, a reference to a memory location includes a value that identifies a segment and an offset (memory location) within that segment. Segments or sections are also used in object files of compiled programs when they are linked together into a program image which then can be loaded into memory.

Segments usually correspond to natural divisions of a program such as individual routines or data tables, so segmentation is generally more visible to the programmer than paging alone. Different segments may be created for different program modules, or for different classes of memory usage such as code and data segments. Certain segments may be shared between programs.

In a system using segmentation, computer memory addresses consist of a segment id and an offset within the segment. A hardware memory management unit (MMU) is responsible for translating the segment and offset into a physical address, and for performing checks to make sure the translation can be done and that the reference to that segment and offset is permitted.

Each segment has a length and will normally have a set of permissions (for example, *read*, *write*, *execute*) associated with it. A process would only be allowed to make a reference into a segment if the type of reference is allowed by the permissions, and if the offset within the segment is within the range specified by the length of the segment. Otherwise, a hardware exception, such as a segmentation fault, would be raised.

Segments may also be used to implement virtual memory. In this case, the MMU would have a segment table (similar to the page table described above[18].) Each segment entry would have an associated flag indicating whether it is present in main memory or not. If a segment is accessed that is not present in main memory, an exception would be raised, and the operating system would read the segment into memory from secondary storage.

Segmentation has been implemented in several different ways on different hardware, with or without paging.

6.3.1   Intel x86 memory segmentation

Intel x86 memory segmentation does not fit either model. The memory segmentation used by early x86 processors, beginning with the Intel 8086, does not provide any protection. Any program running on these processors can access any segment with no restrictions. A segment is only identified by its starting location; there is no length checking, which, obviously, creates serious security issues. Segmentation in the Intel 80286 and later does provide protection

6.3.2   Virtual Memory with Segmentation

Virtual memory with segmentation functions much the same was as virtual memory with paging. Process code and data are subdivided into *segments* which can be stored on disk, loaded individually into RAM as needed, and copied back to secondary storage when it would seem they would not be referenced soon. Thus, segments in a virtual memory system with segments, are treated much as pages are treated in a paging virtual memory system.

Since segments tend to correspond to logical subdivisions in a program rather than physical subdivisions in data storage, there will be less reading and writing back and forth in a segmented virtual memory system than in a paging system. (Most of the code will be compiled into the same segment, and thus all coding references will generally be to commands in the same segment, all of which would be loaded into RAM together. Similarly, related data would tend to be contained in the same segment and would also all loaded together.) segmentation systems, then, will be much less subject to thrashing than will paging systems.

---

[18]   Paging can, in fact, be combined with segmentation.

On the other hand, because segments are not of uniform size, virtual memory systems using segmentation are subject to fragmentation of their primary storage systems. There are techniques for avoiding, or reducing such

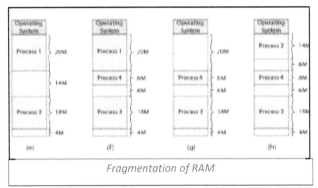

Fragmentation of RAM

fragmentation, but these all add significantly to the MMU overhead.

6.4 Cache Memory

The principle of locality can be applied in the other direction as well.

New technology was being developed that permitted the creation of RAM that supported faster and faster memory references. Unfortunately, this new faster RAM was also much more expensive. It was not (and still is not) cost effective to build computers in which all of the RAM used the high speed technology, but it was, and is, possible to include a relatively small amount of high speed RAM (called a cache.)

If a CPU references a cell in a given section of RAM, then it is likely that the next few memory references will also be to cells in that same section. This motivated the development of systems that use small segments of high speed RAM (caches.) The contents of blocks of RAM containing sections likely to be referenced soon are copied into these caches.

These systems permit the effective use of high speed but expensive forms of RAM. If a CPU references a cell in a given section of cache, then it is likely that the next few memory references will also be to cells in that same section. If the processor references a location in normal RAM, the section of memory containing that cell weould be copied into the cache, and, by the principle of locality, the next several memory references would probably be made using the high speed RAM in the cache. In this way, although only using only a small amount of memory with high speed technology, most of the CPU operations would be executed using that high speed memory.

Of course, in systems with cache memory, the operating system has the additional responsibility of keeping track of which memory sections are duplicated in cache, which sections have been referenced recently, and which cache cells have had their contents modified (and must therefore be copied back to regular RAM before being replaced by more recently accessed memory sections.)

Just as with virtual memory, cache memory systems are subject to thrashing, and effective replacement strategies are critical to their success.

6.4.1 Blocks

Cache memory uses a technique similar to paging, but, caches tend to be rather smaller than pages. The cache is divided into standard sized sections, called *blocks*.

When a process references an address, the system first checks to see if that address is already represented in cache. If it is not, the system will try to find an empty block in cache. If there is no unused block, the system will choose one of the blocks to overwrite. The contents of a section RAM the size of a block and containing the referenced address will be copied into the selected block in cache, and the process resumes execution, using the contents of words stored in cache and not those in RAM. As with virtual memory, if a block must be overwritten, there are several algorithms used to choose which one to overwrite.

6.4.2 Values in Cache that have been Modified

A factor that must be taken into consideration in choosing a block to remove from cache is whether the contents of the block have been modified. When cache data has been modified, it must be copied back to RAM before the block can be overwritten, or information will be lost. Clearly this takes more time than simply copying new data into the cache block.

Further, if data in a cache block has been modified, there exists the possibility that another process might attempt to reference the same data (whose cache version has been modified.) There are three ways this could play out:

The system might keep a record of which blocks are in cache, and allow the second process to also reference the copy of data in cache. This system requires extra (high speed) memory for these records, and each memory reference by the processor must be processed using this record. This would clearly not be an option for multiprocessor systems in which processors do not all share all of their caches.

The system might copy any modified data back to RAM as soon as it is modified in cache, so that the information in cache is always a faithful representation of the corresponding block in RAM. This technique requires many write operations from cache to RAM, and reduces the effectiveness of the use of cache, especially for processes that make frequent modifications to contents of memory cells.

The system might permit the second process to access the data as it appears in RAM (which in this scenario, would not be the "correct" information as calculated by the first process. i.e. would be "dirty" data)

6.4.3   Cache Replacement Algorithms

cache algorithms (also frequently called cache replacement algorithms or cache replacement policies) are **algorithms** that a **program** or a hardware-maintained structure can use to manage a **cache** of information stored on the computer. When the cache is full, the algorithm must choose which items to discard to make room for the new ones.

There are two primary measures used for the management of a cache: The *latency*, and the *hit rate*. There are also a number of secondary factors affecting cache performance.

Hit Rate: The "hit rate" (or "hit ratio") of a cache describes how often a searched-for item is actually found in the cache. More efficient replacement policies keep track of more usage information in order to improve the hit rate (for a given cache size) Hit rate measurements are typically performed **on benchmark** applications. The actual hit ratio varies widely from one application to another. In particular, video and audio streaming applications often have a hit ratio close to zero, because each bit of data in the stream is read once for the first time (a compulsory miss), used, and then never reLaid or written again. Even worse, many cache algorithms (in particular, LRU) allow this streaming data to fill the cache, pushing out of the cache information that will be used again soon (**cache pollution**).

Latency: The "latency" of a cache describes how long after requesting a desired item the cache can return that item (when there is a hit). Faster replacement strategies typically keep track of less usage information—or, in the case of direct-mapped cache, no information—to reduce the amount of time required to update that information.

Each replacement strategy is a compromise between hit rate and latency.

Other factors that might be considered include:

- Items with different cost: keep items that are expensive to obtain, e.g. those that take a long time to get.

- Items taking up more cache: If items have different sizes, the cache may want to discard a large item to provide space to store several smaller ones.

- Items that expire with time: Some caches keep information that expires (e.g. a news cache, a DNS cache, or a web browser cache). The computer may discard items because they are expired. Depending on the size of the cache no further caching algorithm to discard items may be necessary.

Replacement Policies for cache are, for the most part, very similar to those for virtual memory:

FIFO (First in first out) Using this algorithm the cache behaves in the same way as a FIFO queue. The cache evicts the first block accessed first without any regard to how often or how many times it was accessed before. FIFO is simple to implement and has very low overhead.

LRU (Least recently used) Discards the least recently used items first. This algorithm requires keeping track of what was used when This is expensive if one wants to make sure the algorithm *always* discards the least recently used item. General implementations of this technique require keeping "age bits" for cache-lines and track the "Least Recently Used" cache-line based on age-bits. In such an implementation, every time a cache-line is used, the age of all other cache-lines changes.

PLRU (Pseudo LRU) For larger caches, the implementation cost of LRU becomes prohibitive. In many CPU caches, a scheme that usually discards one of the less recently used items is sufficient. So many CPU designers choose a PLRU algorithm which only needs one bit per cache item to work. PLRU typically has a slightly worse miss ratio, has a slightly better latency, uses slightly less power than LRU and lower overheads compared to LRU.

TLRU (Time aware least recently used) The Time aware Least Recently Used is a variant of LRU designed for the situation where the stored contents in cache have a valid life time. The algorithm is suitable in some network cache applications, and especially for distributed networks.

MRU (Most recently used) In contrast to LRU, discards the *most* recently used items first. It has been shown[19] that when a file is being repeatedly scanned in a looping sequential pattern, MRU is the best replacement algorithm." MRU algorithms are, of course, most useful in situations where the older an item is, the more likely it is to be accessed.

RR (Random replacement) Randomly selects a candidate item and discards it to make space when necessary. This algorithm does not require keeping any information about the access history. For its simplicity, it has been used in ARM processors.

---

[19] By Chou and DeWitt in findings presented at the 11th VLDB conference

LFU (Least-frequently used) Counts how often an item is needed. Those that are used least often are discarded first. This works very similar to LRU except that instead of storing the value of how recently a block was accessed, we store the value of how many times it was accessed.

LFUDA (LFU with Dynamic Aging) LFUDA uses dynamic aging to accommodate shifts in the set of popular objects. It adds a cache age factor to the reference count when a new object is added to the cache or when an existing object is re-referenced. LFUDA increments the cache ages when removing blocks. If an object was frequently accessed in the past and now it becomes unpopular, the newly or less popular objects would be allowed to replace it.

6.4.4 Cache Memory Associativity[xxii]

The replacement policy decides where in the cache a copy of a particular entry of main memory will go. If the replacement policy is free to choose any entry in the cache to hold the copy, the cache is called *fully associative*. At the other extreme, if each entry in main memory can go in just one place in the cache, the cache is *direct mapped*. Many caches implement a compromise in which each entry in main memory can go to any one of N places in the cache, and are described as N-way set associative. For example, the level-1 data cache in an AMD Athlon is two-way set associative, which means that any particular location in main memory can be cached in either of two locations in the level-1 data cache.

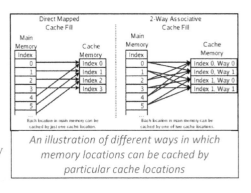

An illustration of different ways in which memory locations can be cached by particular cache locations

Choosing the right value of associativity involves a **trade-off**. If there are ten places to which the replacement policy could have mapped a memory location, then to check if that location is in the cache, ten cache entries must be searched. Checking more places takes more power and chip area, and potentially more time. On the other hand, caches with more associativity suffer fewer misses so that the CPU wastes less time reading from the slow main memory. The general guideline is that doubling the associativity, from direct mapped to two-way, or from two-way to four-way, has about the same effect on raising the hit rate as doubling the cache size. However, increasing associativity more than four does not improve hit rate as much, and are generally done for other reasons.

In order of worse but simple to better but complex:

- Direct mapped cache – good best-case time, but flaky in worst case

- Two-way set associative cache

- Two-way skewed associative cache

- Four-way set associative cache

- Eight-way set associative cache, a common choice for later implementations

- 12-way set associative cache, similar to eight-way

- Fully associative cache – the best miss rates, but practical only for a small number of entries

6.4.4.1 Direct Mapped Cache

With this cache organization, each location in main memory can go in only one entry in the cache. Therefore, a direct-mapped cache can also be called a "one-way set associative" cache. It does not have a replacement policy as such, since there is no choice of which cache entry's contents to evict. This means that if two locations map to the same entry, they may continually knock each other out. Although simpler, a direct-mapped cache needs to be much larger than an associative one to give comparable performance, and it is more unpredictable. Let x be block number in cache, y be block number of memory, and n be number of blocks in cache, then mapping is done with the help of the equation $x = y \bmod n$.

6.4.4.2 Two-Way Set Associative Cache

If each location in main memory can be cached in either of two locations in the cache, one logical question is: *which one of the two?* The simplest and most commonly used scheme, shown in the right-hand diagram above, is to use the least significant bits of the memory location's index as the index for the cache memory, and to have two entries for each index. One benefit of this scheme is that the tags stored in the cache do not have to include that part of the main memory address which is implied by the cache memory's index. Since the cache tags have fewer bits, they require fewer transistors, take less space on the processor circuit board or on the microprocessor chip, and can be read and compared faster. Also, LRU is especially simple since only one bit needs to be stored for each pair

6.4.4.3 Speculative Execution[20]

One of the advantages of a direct mapped cache is that it allows simple and fast **speculation**. Once the address has been computed, the one cache index which might have a copy of that location in memory is known. That cache entry can be read, and the processor can continue to work with that data before it finishes checking that the tag actually matches the requested address.

The idea of having the processor use the cached data before the tag match completes can be applied to associative caches as well. A subset of the tag, called a *hint*, can be used to pick just one of the possible cache entries mapping to the requested address. The entry selected by the hint can then be used in parallel with checking the full tag. The hint technique works best when used in the context of address translation, as explained below

6.4.5 Cache Miss

A cache miss is a failed attempt to read or write a piece of data in the cache, which results in a main memory access with much longer latency. There are three kinds of cache misses: instruction read miss, data read miss, and data write miss.

Cache read misses from an *instruction* cache generally cause the largest delay, because the processor, or at least the thread of execution, has to wait (stall) until the instruction is fetched from main memory.

Cache read misses from a *data* cache usually cause a smaller delay, because instructions not dependent on the cache read can be issued and continue execution until the data is returned from main memory, and the dependent instructions can resume execution.

Cache write misses to a *data* cache generally cause the shortest delay, because the write can be queued and there are few limitations on the execution of subsequent instructions; the processor can continue until the queue is full.

---

[20] **Speculative execution** is an optimization technique where a computer system performs some task that may not be needed. Work is done before it is known whether it is actually needed, so as to prevent a delay that would have to be incurred by doing the work after it is known that it is needed. If it turns out the work was not needed after all, most changes made by the work are reverted and the results are ignored

6.5 Questions

6.5.1 True-False

6.5.1.1 RAM is much cheaper than external storage

6.5.1.2 Virtual memory adds to the complexity of the operating systems

6.5.1.3 The CPU can only deal directly with locations in primary storage.

6.5.1.4 When a process begins execution in a virtual memory system implemented by paging, all of the pages containing sections of the process must be called into memory in order to establish a system of virtual addresses to be used in executing the process.

6.5.1.5 Locality of reference has strengthened for user software. This is mostly attributed to the spread of object-oriented programming techniques that emphasize unified structures.

6.5.1.6 Page replacement in modern kernels (Linux, FreeBSD, and Solaris) tends to work at the level of a general purpose kernel memory allocator, rather than at the higher level of a virtual memory subsystem.

6.5.1.7 Pages usually correspond to natural divisions of a program such as individual routines or data tables, so paging is generally more visible to the programmer than segmentation

6.5.1.8 Segmentation is incompatible with virtual memory

6.5.1.9 Virtual memory systems using segmentation will be much less subject to thrashing than will paging systems

6.5.1.10 Replacement policies for cache are, for the most part, quite different from those for virtual memory

6.5.2 Multiple Choice

6.5.2.1 Virtual memory systems are subject to _____, which occurs when the computer's virtual memory resources become saturated, leading to a constant state of exchanging data in memory for data on disk,
a. whiplash
b. thrashing
c. rocking
d. bouncing
e. none of the above

6.5.2.2 There are a number of possible strategies for choosing a page to swap out. One of them, _____ is relatively easy to implement. Unfortunately, in many systems this algorithm has been seen to target popular library functions used by many processes
a. CLOCK
b. LFU
c. NRU
d. FIFO
e. none of the above

6.5.2.3 The replacement policy decides where in the cache a copy of a particular entry of main memory will go. If the replacement policy is free to choose any entry in the cache to hold the copy, the cache is called _____ *associative*.
a. *completely*
b. *totally*
c. *fully*
d. *entirely*
e. none of the above

6.5.3 Completion

6.5.3.1 Systems can use disk space as an extension of their memory space (_____ memory systems)

6.5.3.2 The principle of locality states that memory references by the processor tend to _____

6.5.3.3 The time it takes for the desired sector to rotate to a position under the read/write head is called rotational _____

6.5.3.4 In a paging system, a program references a word by means of a(n) _____ *address*, which is implemented as a *page number* and an *offset* within the page

6.5.3.5   There are a number of possible strategies for choosing a page to swap out. With one of them, _____ page references closer to the current time have more impact than earlier page references. This ensures that pages referenced more recently, even though less frequently, will have higher priority over pages frequently referenced in the past

6.5.3.6   Memory _____ is the division of a computer's primary memory sections. Unlike pages which are not generally of uniform sizes, and are generally controlled by programmers, rather than the operating system

6.5.3.7   It is not cost effective to build computers in which all of the RAM is of high speed technology, but it is possible to include a relatively small section using high speed RAM (such a section is called a _____.)

6.5.3.8   _____ **execution** is an optimization technique where a computer system performs some task that may not be needed

7. Organization of Information

Computers are digital devices and information is represented in binary format, using 0's or 1's (bits.)

Since the amount of information that can be represented using a single bit is so limited, computing systems typically use *combinations* of bits (0's or 1's)

Some of these combinations are known as bytes, words, doublewords, blocks, pages, files, and directories. Each is used to represent and or manipulate some kinds of information, in several cases many different kinds of information.

7.1 Bytes

The **byte** as a unit of digital information most commonly consists of eight bits. Historically, the byte was the number of bits used to encode a single character of text in a computer and in many computer architectures, the term has often been used to mean the smallest addressable unit of memory.

The size of the byte has historically been hardware dependent and no definitive standards existed that mandated the size (byte-sizes from 1 to 48 bits are known to have been used in the past.) Early character encoding systems often used six bits, and machines using six-bit and nine-bit bytes were common into the 1960s. These machines most commonly had memory words of 12, 24, 36, 48 or 60 bits, corresponding to two, four, six, eight or 10 six-bit bytes.

The modern *de-facto* standard of eight bits (as documented in ISO/IEC 2382-1:1993) is a convenient power of two permitting, as decimal integers, the values 0 through 255 for one byte. Many types of applications use information representable in eight or fewer bits and processor designers optimize for this common usage. The popularity of major commercial computing architectures has aided in the ubiquitous acceptance of the eight-bit size.

The development of **eight-bit microprocessors** in the 1970s popularized this storage size. Microprocessors such as the **Intel 8008** (the direct predecessor of the **8080 and the 8086**) used in early personal computers, could also perform a small number of operations on the **four-bit** pairs in a byte (such as the decimal-add-adjust DAA instruction.) A four-bit quantity is often called a nibble, also *nybble*, which is conveniently represented by a single hexadecimal digit.

Many programming languages define the data type *byte*.

In data transmission systems, the byte is defined as a contiguous sequence of bits in a serial data stream representing the smallest distinguished unit of data. A transmission unit might include start bits, stop bits, or parity bits, and thus could vary from 7 to 12 bits to contain a single 7-bit ASCII code

Each byte in memory will have an address, identifying its location, and each combination of bytes (each word, etc.) will also have an address derived from the bytes from which it is constituted.

7.2 Words (and Doublewords)

In computing, a **word** is the natural unit of data used by a particular processor design. A word is a fixed-sized piece of data handled as a unit by the instruction set or the hardware of the processor. The number of bits in a word (the *word size*, *word width*, or *word length*) is an important characteristic of any specific processor design or computer architecture.

Modern architectures typically use 32 or 64-bit words, built of four or eight bytes.

The size of a word is reflected in many aspects of a computer's structure and operation; the majority of the registers in a processor are usually word sized and the largest piece of data that can be transferred to and from the working memory in a single operation is a word in many (not all) architectures. The largest possible address size, used to designate a location in memory, is typically a hardware word (here, "hardware word" means the full-sized natural word of the processor, as opposed to any other definition used).

Modern processors, including embedded systems, usually have a word size of 8, 16, 24, 32, or 64 bits, while modern general purpose computers usually use 32 or 64 bits. Special purpose digital processors may use other sizes, and many other sizes have been used historically, including 9, 12, 18, 24, 26, 36, 39, 40, 48, and 60 bits. Several of the earliest computers (and a few modern as well) used binary-coded decimal rather than plain binary, typically having a word size of 10 or 12 decimal digits, and some early decimal computers had no fixed word length at all.

The size of a word can sometimes differ from the expected due to backward compatibility with earlier computers. If multiple compatible variations or a family of processors share a common architecture and instruction set but differ in their word sizes, their documentation and software may become notationally complex to accommodate the difference.

7.3 Cache Blocks/Cache Lines

A *cache* is a section of smaller, faster memory, which stores copies of the data from frequently used main memory locations. Most CPUs have different independent caches, including instruction and data caches. The data cache is usually organized as a hierarchy of more cache levels (L1, L2, etc.).

Data is transferred between memory and cache in blocks of fixed size, called *cache lines* or *cache blocks*. When a cache line is copied from memory into the cache, a cache entry is created. The cache entry will include the copied data as well as an identification (called a tag) of the location in main memory that the block/line is a copy of.

Cache row entries usually have the following structure:

tag	data block	flag bits

When the processor needs to read or write a location in main memory, it first checks for a corresponding entry in the cache. The cache checks for the contents of the requested memory location in any cache lines that might contain that address. If the processor finds that the memory location is in the cache, a cache hit has occurred. However, if the processor does not find the memory location in the cache, a cache miss has occurred. In the case of a cache hit, the processor immediately reads or writes the data in the cache line. For a cache miss, the cache allocates a new entry and copies data from main memory, then the request is fulfilled from the contents of the cache.

Example

The original Pentium 4 had a 4-way set associative L1 data cache of size 8 KB with 64 byte cache blocks. Hence, there are 8KB/64 = 128 cache blocks. If it's 4-way set associative, this implies 128/4=32 sets (and hence $2^5 = 32$ different indices). There are $64=2^6$ possible offsets. Since the CPU address is 32 bits, this implies $32=21+5+6$, and hence 21 bits of tag field.

The original Pentium 4 also had an 8-way set associative L2 integrated cache of size 256 KB with 128 byte cache blocks. This implies $32=17+8+7$, and hence 17 bits of tag field.

As indicated above, different systems will have cache blocks of different sizes (and, in fact different caches on the same system will use blocks of different sizes.)

7.4   Pages

With the development of virtual memory systems (and disk cache systems) it became desirable to divide system RAM into sections of uniform sizes related to amount of information that could be conveniently (and relatively efficiently) read from and/or written to a hard disk. These subdivisions became to be referred to as "*pages*"

7.4.1 Tracks and Sectors[xxiii]

In computer disk storage, a **sector** is a subdivision of a **track** on a magnetic disk or optical disc. Each sector stores a fixed amount of user-accessible data, (traditionally 512 bytes for hard disk drives and 2048 bytes for CD-ROMs and DVD-ROMs. Newer HDDs use 4096-byte sectors, which are known as the Advanced Format, *AF*).

The sector is the minimum storage unit of a hard drive. Most disk partitioning schemes are designed to have files occupy an integral number of sectors regardless of the file's actual size. Files that do not fill a whole sector will have the remainder of their last sector filled with zeroes.

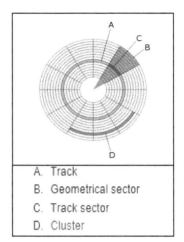

A. Track
B. Geometrical sector
C. Track sector
D. Cluster

7.4.2 Page Sizes[xxiv]

The process of reading from or writing to a disk involves two steps, first moving the read/write head to the correct track, and then waiting until the desired sector rotates into position to be read from or written to. Moving the head to the correct track generally takes more time (latency) than it does for the sector to arrive to the read/write head (rotational delay) and so it is efficient (takes less data transfer time) to store data that tends to be referenced together on the same track.

Computer	Page Size
Atlas	512 48-bit words
Honeywell-Multics	1024 36-bit words
IBM 370/XA and 370/ESA	4 Kbytes
VAX family	512 bytes
IBM AS/400	512 bytes
DEC Alpha	8 Kbytes
MIPS	4 Kbytes to 16 Mbytes
UltraSPARC	8 Kbytes to 4 Mbytes
Pentium	4 Kbytes or 4 Mbytes
IBM POWER	4 Kbytes
Itanium	4 Kbytes to 256 Mbytes
Some Page Sizes	

It is the basic idea of virtual memory systems to store and load sections of data that will be referenced together. It makes sense to store and load data together as pages onto and from the same track, and so pages will be multiples of the sector size used on hard disks on the system.

7.5 Segments

Memory segmentation is the division of a computer's primary memory into **segments** or **sections**. In a computer system using segmentation, a reference to a memory location includes a value that identifies a segment and an offset (memory location) within that segment.

Segments usually correspond to natural divisions of a program such as individual routines or data tables, so segmentation is generally more visible to the programmer than paging. Different segments may be created for different program modules, or for different classes of memory usage such as code and data segments. Segments might also be shared between programs.

7.6   Files, Directories, Subdirectories, File Manager

A **computer file** is a computer resource for recording data discretely in a computer storage device. Just as words can be written to paper, so can information be written to a computer file.

There are different types of computer files, designed for different purposes. A file may be designed to store a picture, a written message, a video, a computer program, or a wide variety of other kinds of data. Some types of files can store several types of information at once (multimedia files for example.)

By using computer programs, a person can open, read, change, and close a computer file. Computer files may be reopened, modified, and copied an arbitrary number of times.

Typically, files are organized in a file system, which keeps track of where the files are located on disk and enables user access.

On most modern operating systems, files are organized into one-dimensional arrays of bytes. The format of a file is defined by its content since a file is solely a container for data. On some platforms, however, the file format is dictated by its filename extension which will specifying the rules for how the bytes in the file must be organized and interpreted.

For example, the bytes of a plain text file (.txt in Windows) are associated with either ASCII or UTF-8 characters, while the bytes of image, video, and audio files are interpreted in other ways.

Most file types also allocate a few bytes for metadata[21], which allows a file to carry some basic information about itself.

Information in a computer file can consist of smaller packets of information (often called "records" or "lines") that are individually different but share some common traits. For example, a payroll file might contain information concerning all the employees in a company and their payroll details; each record in the payroll file concerns just one employee, and all the records

---

[21]   Metadata is data [information] that provides information about other data

have the common trait of being related to payroll—this is very similar to placing all payroll information into a specific filing cabinet in an office that does not have a computer. A text file may contain lines of text, corresponding to printed lines on a piece of paper. Alternatively, a file may contain an arbitrary binary image (a BLOB) or it may contain an executable[22].

The most basic operations that programs can perform on a file are:

- Create a new file
- Change the access permissions and attributes of a file
- Open a file, which makes the file contents available to the program
- Read data from a file
- Write data to a file
- Close a file, terminating the association between it and the program

7.7 RAID Systems

When relatively inexpensive, albeit smaller and, in many cases less reliable, hard disks started to be marketed, it was recognized that by using several smaller hard disks instead of just one large disk, one could use a collection of smaller less expensive disks to create a *system* having a large capacity. Such a system could have several advantages:

Price: It was usually possible to buy large storage capacity for less money as a combination of smaller cheaper drives than a single high capacity drive would cost, since the smaller drives were manufactured in large quantities, resulting in economies of scale. The smaller drives were also more readily available.

Reliability: With several different drives, it is possible to put duplicate data on more than one drive. Then, if one drive were to fail, its data would not be lost.

Access Speed: With data in a large file stored on different drives, the system can read different portions of the file from the different drives simultaneously, resulting in faster upload times than would be possible with one single drive.

---

[22] In computing, **executable code** or an **executable file** or **executable program**, sometimes simply referred to as an **executable** or **binary**, causes a computer "to perform indicated tasks according to encoded instructions," as opposed to a data file that must be parsed by some program to be meaningful.

In a RAID system, data can be distributed across the drives in several different ways, referred to as RAID levels. These levels vary according to the required level of redundancy and performance.

The different schemes, or data distribution layouts, are named by the word RAID followed by a number, for example RAID 0 or RAID 1.

Each scheme, or RAID level, provides a different balance among the key goals: reliability, availability, performance, and capacity.

RAID levels greater than RAID 0 provide protection against unrecoverable sector read errors, as well as against failures of whole physical drives

7.7.1 RAID 0 Striping[xxv]

RAID 0 has no redundancy, and so does not provide improved reliability. It does, however, provide improved access speed.

A large file would be divided into several different *stripes*. Different strips would be stored on different drives. When uploading or downloading the file multiple strips could be uploaded/downloaded simultaneously, resulting in much improved I/O rates.

A RAID 0 array of *n* drives provides data read and write transfer rates up to *n* times as high as the individual drive rates, but with no data redundancy. As a result, RAID 0 is primarily used in applications that require high performance and are able to tolerate lower reliability, such as in scientific computing or computer gaming.

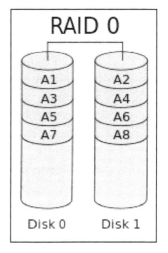

7.7.2 RAID 1 Mirroring[xxvi]

RAID 1 consists of having exact copies/mirrors of a set of data on two or more disks. In the illustration, there are two copies of one disk, but there can be more disk (ie for either disk, we could substitute another RAID system.)

RAID 1 does not use parity or striping across the mirrored disks. This layout is useful when read performance or reliability is more important than write performance or the resulting data storage capacity.

The array will continue to operate so long as at least one member drive is operational.

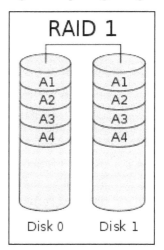

Any read request can be serviced and handled by any drive in the array; thus, depending on the nature of I/O load, random read performance of a RAID 1 array may be as good as the sum of each member's performance (different portions of a file can be read from different disks, simultaneously, but the write performance remains at the level of a single disk, since a write operation must go to both disks (although simultaneously.)

RAID 1 systems require twice as many disks as do RAID 0 systems to achieve the same storage capacity.

7.7.3 RAID 2 Bit Level Striping with Parity[xxvii]

RAID 2, which is rarely used in practice, stripes data at the bit (rather than block) level, and uses a Hamming code for error correction. The disks are synchronized by the controller to spin at the same angular orientation and it generally cannot service multiple requests simultaneously. Extremely high data transfer rates are possible.

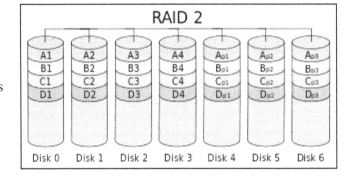

With all hard disk drives implementing internal error correction, the complexity of an external Hamming code offered little advantage over parity so RAID 2 has been rarely implemented; it is the only original level of RAID that is not currently used.

7.7.4 RAID 3 Byte Level Striping with Parity Disk[xxviii]

RAID 3, which is rarely used in practice, consists of byte-level striping with a dedicated parity disk. One of the characteristics of RAID 3 is that it generally cannot service multiple requests simultaneously. This is because any single block of data will be

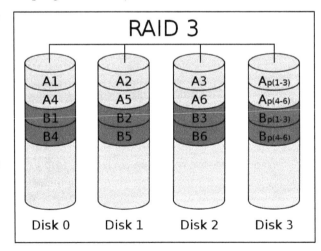

spread across all members of the set and will be positioned in the same location. Therefore, virtually any I/O operation requires activity on every disk (and usually requires synchronized spindles, as well.)

This makes RAID 3 suitable for applications that demand the highest transfer rates in long sequential reads and writes (video editing, for example.) Applications that make small reads and writes from random disk locations will get the worst performance out of this level.

This level provides no significant advantages over other RAID levels, so it is, in fact, now obsolete. Both RAID 3 and RAID 4 were quickly replaced by RAID 5.

7.7.5 RAID 4 Block Level Striping with Parity Disk[xxix]

RAID 4 consists of block-level striping with a dedicated parity disk. RAID 4 provides good performance of reads, but the performance doing writes is low because of the need to write all parity data to a single disk.

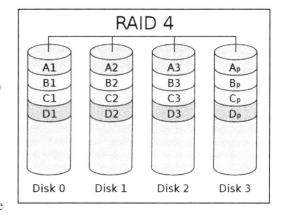

In the diagram, a read request for block A1 would be serviced by disk 0. A simultaneous read request for block B1 would have to wait, but a read request for B2 could be serviced concurrently by disk 1.

7.7.6 RAID 5 block-level striping with distributed parity[xxx]

RAID 5 consists of block-level striping with distributed parity. Unlike in RAID 4, parity information is distributed among the drives. It requires that all drives but one be present to operate. Upon failure of a single drive, subsequent reads can be calculated from the distributed parity such that no data is lost. RAID 5 requires at least three disks.

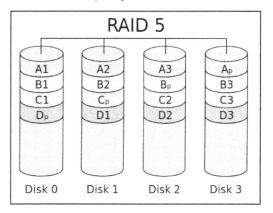

In comparison to RAID 4, RAID 5's distributed parity evens out the stress of a dedicated parity disk among all RAID members. Additionally, write performance is increased since all RAID members participate in the serving of write requests. Although it won't be as efficient as a striping (RAID 0) setup, because parity must still be written, this is no longer a bottleneck.

Since parity calculation is performed on the full stripe, small changes to the array experience *write amplification*: in the worst case when a single, logical sector is to be written, the original sector and the according parity sector need to be read, the original data is removed from the parity, the new data calculated into the parity and both the new data sector and the new parity sector are written.

7.7.7 RAID 6 block-level striping with two parity blocks[xxxi]

RAID 6 extends RAID 5 by adding another parity block; so, it uses block-level striping with two parity blocks distributed across all member disks.

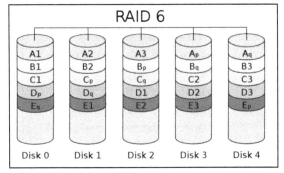

According to the Storage Networking Industry Association (SNIA), the definition of RAID 6 is: "Any form of RAID that can continue to execute read and write requests to all of a RAID array's virtual disks in the presence of any two concurrent disk failures. Several methods, including dual check data computations (parity and Reed-Solomon[23]), orthogonal dual parity check data and diagonal parity, have been used to implement RAID Level 6."

RAID 6 does not have a performance penalty for read operations, but it does have a performance penalty on write operations because of the overhead associated with parity calculations. Performance varies greatly depending on how RAID 6 is implemented in the manufacturer's storage architecture—in software, firmware, or by using firmware and specialized ASICs for intensive parity calculations. RAID 6 can read up to the same speed as RAID 5 with the same number of physical drives.

---

[23] **Reed–Solomon codes** are a group of error-correcting codes that were introduced by Irving S. Reed and Gustave Solomon in 1960. They have many applications, the most prominent of which include consumer technologies such as CDs, DVDs, Blu-ray Discs, QR Codes, data transmission technologies such as DSL and WiMAX, broadcast systems such as DVB and ATSC, and storage systems such as RAID 6. They are also used in satellite communication

7.8   Questions

7.8.1   True-False

7.8.1.1   The size of the byte has historically been hardware dependent and no definitive standards existed that mandated the size

7.8.1.2   Most disk partitioning schemes are designed to optimize disk storage capacity. Each file occupies only the portions of sectors required by data in the file.

7.8.1.3   RAID 0 systems require twice as many disks as do RAID 1 systems to achieve the same storage capacity

7.8.2   Multiple Choice

7.8.2.1   A *word* is a fixed-sized piece of data handled as a unit by the instruction set or the hardware of the processor. The number of bits in a word (the word _____) is an important characteristic of any specific processor design or computer architecture
a.   size
b.   width
c.   length
d.   any of the above
e.   none of the above

7.8.2.2   RAID _____ has no redundancy, and so does not provide improved reliability. It does, however, provide improved access speed.
a.   0
b.   1
c.   4
d.   5
e.   none of the above

7.8.2.3   RAID _____ provides good performance of reads, but the performance doing writes is low because of the need to write all parity data to a single disk
a.   0
b.   1
c.   4
d.   5
e.   none of the above

7.8.2.4   RAID _____ uses block-level striping with two parity blocks distributed across all member disks
   a.   0
   b.   1
   c.   4
   d.   5
   e.   none of the above

7.8.3   Completion

7.8.3.1   Computers are _____ devices and information is represented in binary format

7.8.3.2   The _____ as a unit of digital information most commonly consists of eight bits. Historically, it was the number of bits used to encode a single character of text in a computer and in many computer architectures, the term has often been used to mean the smallest addressable unit of memory

7.8.3.3   In computing, a(n) _____ is the natural unit of data used by a particular processor design.

7.8.3.4   A data cache is usually organized as a(n) _____ of cache levels: (L1, L2, etc.).

7.8.3.6   When the processor needs to read or write a location in main memory, it first checks for a corresponding entry in the cache. The cache checks for the contents of the requested memory location in any cache lines that might contain that address. If the processor finds that the memory location is in the cache, a cache _____ has occurred. In this case, the processor immediately reads or writes the data in the cache line

7.8.3.7   In computer disk storage, a(n) _____ is a subdivision of a **track** on a magnetic disk or optical disc

7.8.3.8   On some platforms the file format is dictated by its filename _____

7.8.3.9   _____ is **data** [information] that provides information about other data

8. Security and Antivirus, Encryption and Decryption

Our daily lives, economic safety, and even national security have come to depend on stable, safe, and resilient computer and communication systems. Thus, computer security is an extremely important issue.

By computer security, we basically mean the maintenance of system integrity and the availability and confidentiality of information dealt with by the computer system. The operating system plays a paramount role in the overall security of the system.

8.1 Security Issues

The main security issues that an operating system might be expected to deal with are issues of:

Authenticity

Availability

Confidentiality

Data integrity.

8.2 Sources of Threats to System Security

One of the functions of an operating system is to provide a level of security, and so, the system should should work to defend against:

physical malfunctions

user errors

attacks from external sources.

The security within a computer system can be divided into various layers such as maintaining:

the security of the information the system holds

the physical security of the system,

the security of the network in which it operates.

8.2.1 Physical Malfunctions

The operating system cannot, of course, *prevent* physical malfunctions, so its role in this regard would be limited to *detecting* the malfunctions when they occur[24], and limiting their damage to the information in the system.

---

[24] And they WILL occur.

Data storage is subject to errors, and so is data transmission.

8.2.1.1 Data errors

In a digital system, a data error will take the form of either a 0 stored (or transmitted) when the correct value would have been 1 or a 1 stored/transmitted instead of a 0. Such errors can be due to manufacturing defects, wear, environmental EMF, and many other factors.

8.2.1.1.1 Error Detection and Correction

Most systems utilize forms of error detection, and often and error correction. These techniques enable reliable storage/delivery of digital data. Error *detection* techniques support *detection* of errors, while error *correction* enables *reconstruction* of the original data (at least in many cases.)

8.2.1.1.1.1 Redundancy

The general idea for achieving error detection/correction is to add some **redundancy** (i.e., some extra data) to the data, which users can utilize to check consistency of the data, and, possibly, to recover data that has been corrupted.

In such a scheme, a number of *check bits* (or *parity data*) (derived from the data bits by some **algorithm**) are added to the data. A user can simply apply the same algorithm to the data bits and compare its output with the check bits; if the values do not match, an error must have occurred.

Many such algorithms also support error correction, i.e. they can be used to identify which data bits had erroneous values. (Since the only values are 0 and 1, the correct value is trivially identified. If the data value is 0 and it is wrong, the correct value must have been 1. If the data value is 1 and it is erroneous, then the correct value must be 0.)

8.2.1.1.1.2 Parity bits

A *parity bit* is a bit that is added to a group of source/data bits to ensure that the number of *set* bits (i.e., bits with value 1) in the outcome is even or odd. It is a very simple scheme that can be used to detect single or any other odd number (i.e., three, five, etc.) of errors in the group of data bits. If, however, there is an *even* number of flipped bits, the parity bit would fail to indicate any error, even though the data *is*, in fact, erroneous.

8.2.1.1.1.3 Checksums

A *checksum* of a collection (of a fixed word length) of data is a modular arithmetic sum of that data. Such a sum may be negated by means of a ones'-complement operation, which provides a very efficient operation which will result in all zero data unless there is an error.

Checksum schemes include parity bits, check digits, and longitudinal redundancy checks. Some checksum schemes are specifically designed to detect errors commonly introduced by humans when writing down or remembering identification numbers.

8.2.1.1.1.4 Data Storage

Error detection and correction codes are often used to improve the reliability of data storage media.
(In fact, a "parity track" was present on the first magnetic tape data storage in 1951.)
The "Optimal Rectangular Code" used in group coded recording tapes not only detects but also corrects single-bit errors.
Some file formats, (particularly archive formats), include a checksum (most often CRC32) to detect corruption and truncation and can employ redundancy and/or parity files to recover portions of corrupted data. Reed Solomon codes[25] are used in compact discs to correct errors caused by scratches.

Modern hard drives use CRC codes to detect minor errors in sector reads, and Reed–Solomon codes to correct them. They are also used to recover data from sectors that have "gone bad" and store that data in spare sectors.

RAID systems use a variety of error correction techniques to correct errors when a hard drive completely fails. Some filesystems, as well as some RAID implementations, support data scrubbing[26] and

---

[25] **Reed–Solomon codes** are a group of error-correcting codes that were introduced by Irving S. Reed and Gustave Solomon in 1960. They have many applications, the most prominent of which include consumer technologies such as CDs, DVDs, Blu-ray Discs, QR Codes, data transmission technologies such as DSL and WiMAX, broadcast systems such as DVB and ATSC, and storage systems such as RAID 6. They are also used in satellite communication.

[26] data scrubbing is an error correction technique that uses a background task to periodically inspect main memory or storage for errors, then correct detected errors.

resilvering[27], which allows bad blocks to be detected and (hopefully) recovered before they are used. The recovered data may be re-written to exactly the same physical location, to spare blocks elsewhere on the same piece of hardware, or the data may be rewritten onto replacement hardware.

8.2.1.1.1.5 Error-correcting memory

DRAM memory may provide increased protection by relying on built in error correcting codes. This kind of **error-correcting memory** (known as *ECC* or *EDAC-protected* memory) is particularly desirable for applications, such as servers, which cannot tolerate errors, as well as deep-space applications which suffer relatively high rates of RAM errors due to high **radiation levels**.

Error-correcting memory controllers traditionally use *Hamming codes*, although some use *triple modular redundancy*.

8.2.1.1.1.6 *Interleaving*

Interleaving can ameliorate the effect of a single radiation event, keeping it from modifying multiple bits in physically neighboring words. It associates neighboring bits to different words.

As long as a *single event upset* (SEU) does not exceed the error threshold (e.g., a single error) in any particular word between accesses, it can be corrected, by a single-bit error correcting code, and the illusion of an error-free memory system may be maintained.

8.2.1.1.1.7 Error Reporting

In addition to using hardware that provides features required for ECC memory to operate, **operating systems** usually have reporting facilities that are used to provide notifications when errors are transparently recovered. An increasing rate of such automatically corrected errors might indicate that a DIMM[28] module needs replacing, and such feedback information would not be easily available without the

---

Data scrubbing reduces the likelihood that single correctable errors will accumulate, leading to reduced risks of uncorrectable errors.

[27] Resilvering (also known as resyncing, rebuilding, or reconstructing) is the process of repairing a damaged device using the contents of healthy devices.

[28] **DIMM** or **dual in-line memory module** comprises a series of dynamic random-access memory integrated circuits. These modules are mounted on a printed circuit board and designed for use in personal computers, workstations and servers

related reporting capabilities. One example is the Linux kernel's *EDAC* subsystem (previously known as *bluesmoke*), which collects the data from error-checking-enabled components inside a computer system; beside collecting and reporting back the events related to ECC memory, it also supports other checksumming errors, including those detected on the PCI bus.

A few systems also support *memory scrubbing*.

8.2.1.1.1.8 Memory scrubbing

Memory scrubbing (similar to data scrubbing) consists of reading from each **computer memory** location, correcting **bit errors** (if any) with an error-correcting code (ECC) and, if necessary, writing the corrected data back to the same location.

Because of the high integration density of modern computer memory **chips**, the individual memory cell structures became small enough to be vulnerable to **cosmic rays** and/or **alpha particle** emission. The errors caused by these phenomena are called *soft errors*. Over 8% of DIMM modules experience at least one such correctable error per year, and this can be a problem for **DRAM** and **SRAM** based memories. The probability of a soft error at any individual memory bit is very small. However, together with the large amount of memory modern computers (and especially **servers**) are equipped with, and together with extended periods of **uptime**, the probability of soft errors in the total memory installed is significant.

The information in an **ECC memory** is stored **redundantly** enough to correct single bit error per memory word, which is good enough to support the scrubbing of the memory content. If the **memory controller** scans systematically through the memory, the single bit errors can be detected, the erroneous bit can be determined using the ECC **checksum**, and the corrected data can be written back to the memory.

8.2.1.1.2 Error Recovery

One of the most important aspects of an operating system is an ability to continue to operate when errors have occurred or to resume operation after errors have occurred.

Many techniques are used to facilitate error recovery. These include:

Designing systems to be able to operate without some of its hardware components.

Implementing error detection and correction capabilities.

Storing multiple copies of critical data in separate locations that are unlikely to suffer simultaneous damage.

When computer files contain information that is extremely important, a *back-up* process is used to protect against disasters that might destroy the files. Backing up files simply means making copies of the files in a separate location so that they can be restored if something happens to the computer, or if they are deleted accidentally.

There are many ways to back up files. Most computer systems provide utility programs to assist in the back-up process, which can become very time-consuming if there are many files to safeguard. Files are often copied to removable media such as writable CDs or cartridge tapes. Copying files to another hard disk in the same computer protects against failure of one disk, but if it is necessary to protect against failure or destruction of the entire computer, then copies of the files must be made on other media that can be taken away from the computer and stored in a safe, distant location.

The grandfather-father-son backup method automatically makes three back-ups; the grandfather file is the oldest copy of the file and the son is the current copy.

8.3   User Errors

Humans do things they shouldn't do, sometimes by mistake, sometimes out of ignorance and sometimes intentionally. We can never completely eliminate these human errors, but we can minimize them (or at least contain their effects) with a with a robust user authentication system and user access security system

to ensure that only authorized users have access to the system,

and that the authorized users only have access to resources for which they have approval.

8.3.1   Security incidents involving Human Error

All humans make mistakes:
One of the most intriguing findings from IBM's "2014 Cyber Security Intelligence Index" is that **95 percent of all security incidents involve human error**. Many of these are successful security attacks from external attackers who prey on human weakness in order to lure insiders within organizations to unwittingly provide them with access to sensitive information.

These mistakes are costly since they involve insiders who often have access to the most sensitive information. According to research by Federal Computer Week cited in a recent Vormetric report, the greatest impacts of successful security attacks involving insiders are exposure of sensitive data, theft of intellectual property and the introduction of malware. The research also reported that 59 percent of respondents agree that most information technology security threats that directly result from insiders are the result of innocent mistakes rather than malicious abuse of privileges.

8.3.2 Security Controls

One of the leading errors made by insiders is sending sensitive documents to unintended recipients. This is relatively easy to solve by deploying security controls to monitor sensitive information being leaked out of the organization. Once considered complex to deploy, in recent years vendors have made these controls much easier to implement. This has dramatically reduced the level of user involvement required and increased the use of such controls.

These tools can also prevent users from engaging in inappropriate behavior, such as sending documents home via email or placing them on file-sharing sites or removable media such as USB sticks.

Lost or stolen mobile devices are also a major concern that is exacerbated by the growing trend toward the use of personal devices. Again, there is technology available to help organizations police what happens to data stored on devices that even allows sensitive data to be remotely wiped to prevent it from falling into the wrong hands.

8.3.3 Errors by Skilled Users

Human error is also a factor in other security incidents caused by insiders who are the most trusted and highly skilled, such as system and network administrators. According to IBM's report, some of the most commonly recorded forms of human error caused by such employees are system misconfigurations, poor patch management practices and the use of default names and passwords. There are a number of security controls that organizations should explore to guard against such threats.

8.3.4 Social Engineering

The human interest factor is also being exploited by attackers and plays a large part in successful security attacks seen today, but it is not always attributed to mistakes made by insiders. Many of these attacks involve social engineering techniques to lure individually targeted users into making mistakes. According to Verizon's "2013 Data Breach Investigations Report", 95 percent of advanced and targeted attacks involved spear-phishing scams with emails containing malicious attachments that can cause malware to be downloaded onto the user's computing device. This gives attackers a foothold into the organization from which they can move laterally in search of valuable information, such as intellectual property.

8.3.5 Changing Tactics

There is evidence some that users are perhaps mending their ways and falling prey to such nefarious activity less frequently. Verizon's 2014 report found that the proportion of successful spearfishing security attacks has fallen to 78 percent.

Is this drop because users are becoming more savvy and are less likely to be lured into making such mistakes, or are attackers changing their tactics? It would appear that the latter is true since Verizon's 2014 report found a sizable increase in the use of strategic Web compromises as a method of gaining initial access. Malicious URL links contained in emails have long been a major vector of attacks, but users are becoming much more aware of such tactics — perhaps heeding advice not to trust such links, but rather to type URLs manually into browsers.

8.3.6 Watering Hole Attacks

Today, legitimate websites are increasingly being hacked since they are just the sort of websites that users would routinely trust. However, compromised websites are also being used in attacks that target the interests of specific users or groups. There has also been a particular increase in so-called watering hole attacks — so named because they mimic the tactics of animals lying and waiting for their prey at the watering holes they are likely to visit.

8.3.7 Technology Alone Is Not a Panacea

There are technologies available for organizations to help safeguard themselves against external factors that target individual users in hopes of causing them to make errors.

It is often said that any successful organization must focus on people, processes and technology in that order. Technology provides automated safeguards and processes to determine the series of actions to be taken to achieve a particular end. But even organizations with strong security practices are still vulnerable to human error. Oftentimes, there is insufficient attention paid to the "people" part of the equation. To stem errors made through social engineering and to raise awareness of the potential caused by carelessness, technology and processes must be combined with employee education. This way, employees are aware of the threats they face and the part they are expected to play in guarding against them. Keeping organizations safe relies on constantly educating employees about identifying suspicious communications and new possible risks.

8.3.8   User Access Security in Computing

"User access" refers to the mechanisms by which user gain access to system resources. In a computer system, the Operating System (OS) is the backbone of the computing environment from which all resources are controlled and run. This means that the operating system is at the core of the entire system's security.

Security takes on many layers. Physical security to the computer system itself is one layer. Anyone within physical proximity to the computer can be a threat. Threats can also come from unauthorized access via the web, compromised applications, or poor user habits.

8.3.8.1   Securing User Access Using the Operating System

There are different operating system security measures available to secure user access. We will now examine some of them.

8.3.8.1.1   Limitations on User Accounts

This entails limiting the number of authorized users who have access to the operating system and respective system applications.

Limiting access to the operating system enables better control of system administration, accountability and troubleshooting.

Limiting access to applications ensures access by the right users to the right applications only. The system must constantly be audited to delete accounts of users who for one reason or another have left the company or business. Legacy accounts can be a huge security threat.

8.3.8.1.2   Password Policies

It is important to ensure that access to network servers, operating systems and applications is mandated and controlled using a system of passwords. This is one of many security layers, and one of the most basic forms of user access security to any system.

Enforcing good user password policies with emphasis on strong passwords combinations is key. With so many tools available online, simple passwords are easy to break and lead to system compromise.

Enforcing frequent password changes is also critical. Familiarity can always lead to compromise. If a user's password has been compromised, frequent changes will narrow the window of attack opportunity. Frequent password changes also ensure that legacy accounts do not become weak points in the system.

8.3.8.1.3 User Permissions

Many modern computer systems provide methods for protecting files against accidental and deliberate damage. Computers that allow for multiple users implement *file permissions* to control who may or may not modify, delete, or create files and folders. For example, a given user may be granted only permission to read a file or folder, but not to modify or delete it; or a user may be given permission to read and modify files or folders, but not to execute them. Permissions may also be used to allow only certain users to see the contents of a file or folder.

Permissions protect against unauthorized tampering or destruction of information in files and keep private information confidential from unauthorized users.

Another protection mechanism implemented in many computers is a *read-only flag*. When this flag is turned on for a file (which can be accomplished by a computer program or by a human user), the file can be examined, but it cannot be modified. This flag is useful for critical information that must not be modified or erased, such as special files that are used only by internal parts of the computer system. Some systems also include a *hidden flag* to make certain files invisible; this flag is used by the computer system to hide essential system files that users should not alter.

User permissions are defined simply as who has access to what. Although an application may have many authorized users, they do not all have the same level of access. In other words, some users or groups of users may have restricted access with the ability to only carry out a few functions. They may, for example, only be allowed to navigate within certain areas in an application. Other users may have more advanced privileges, enabling them to have full access to all operations within the system.

Ensuring that users have the minimum required permissions for them to perform their individual functions is the key. Unauthorized access and malicious attacks often need user access authentication. User permissions can determine the success of an attack and the damage extent. Accounts with administrative and super-user access are the most vulnerable.

Limiting access to approved users will not eliminate user errors, but it will tend to limit the effects of these errors, permitting any errors to affect only those resources for which that particular user has authorized access.

8.4 Measures to Protect System Security

Information security involves security of all data, all applications and of the operating system itself. All of these are sometimes in danger.

Threats may be due to mistakes by humans, malicious programs or persons, or, simply, existing system vulnerabilities. The following measures highlight the role of the operating system in maintaining security.

8.4.1 Authentication

Authentication is one of the protective methods used by OS to ensure that the user accessing a program is authorized or legitimate. An OS provides authentication using a number of techniques:

1. User names and passwords - these are names and passwords registered with the operating system to whom it allows access at the time of login.

2. Key Cards - these are physical cards programmed by the OS with unique identifying information that allows the user to login to the system.

3. User attributes - The operating system registers unique physical characteristics of the user (called attributes) to identify him at login. These may include fingerprints, signatures and eye retina patterns.

8.5 Attacks from External Sources

Cyberspace and its underlying infrastructure are vulnerable to a wide range of risk stemming from both physical and cyber threats and hazards. Sophisticated cyber actors and even nation-states regularly attempt to exploit vulnerabilities of digital systems to steal money and information, and are developing capabilities to disrupt, destroy, or threaten the delivery of essential services.

Information security threats come in many different forms. Some of the most common threats today are:

software attacks,

Most computer users have experienced software attacks of some sort. Viruses, worms, phishing attacks, and Trojan horses are a few common examples of software attacks.

theft of intellectual property,

The theft of intellectual property has also been an extensive issue for many businesses, especially those in the IT field.

identity theft,

> Identity theft is the attempt to act as someone else usually to obtain that person's personal information or to take advantage of their access to vital information.

theft of equipment or information,

> Theft of equipment or information is becoming more prevalent today due to the fact that most devices today are mobile, are prone to theft and have also become far more desirable as the amount of data capacity increases.

sabotage,

> Sabotage usually consists of the destruction of an organization's website, often in an attempt to cause loss of confidence on the part of its customers.

and information extortion.

> Information extortion consists of theft of a company's property or information as an attempt to receive a payment in exchange for returning the information or property back to its owner, as with ransomware.

There are many ways to help protect against most of these attacks and one of the most functional is user carefulness. Nevertheless, a well designed OS will provide an extra level of protection against these external threats, as well as against human errors, programming errors and physical malfunctions.

The nature of the threats that concerns a system will vary greatly depending on the circumstances and on who or what organization runs the system, but the primary problem involves controlling *access* to computer systems and the information stored in them

8.6   Questions

8.6.1   True-False

8.6.1.1   By computer security, we basically mean the maintenance of system integrity and the availability and confidentiality of information dealt with by the computer system. The operating system plays a paramount role in the overall security of the system.

8.6.1.2   A parity single bit can detect whether an even number of errors have occurred in a data set, but it will not detect an odd number of errors.

8.6.1.3   Systems have recently begun using error detection and correction codes to improve the reliability of data storage media.

8.6.1.4   Error detection and correction codes are often used to improve the reliability of data storage media. This is not a recent development. In fact, a "parity track" was present on the first magnetic tape data storage in 1951.)

8.6.1.5   Operating systems usually have reporting facilities that are used to provide notifications when errors are transparently recovered.

8.6.1.6   95 percent of all security incidents involve human error

8.6.1.7   Frequent password changes ensure that legacy accounts do not become weak points in the system

8.6.2   Multiple Choice

8.6.2.1   One of the functions of an operating system is to provide a level of security, and so, the system should work to defend against _____
   a.   physical malfunctions
   b.   user errors
   c.   attacks from external sources
   d.   all of the above
   e.   none of the above

8.6.2.2   Because of the high integration density of modern computer memory chips, the individual memory cell structures became small enough to be vulnerable to cosmic rays and/or alpha particle emission. The errors caused by these phenomena are called _____ errors.
   a.   radiation
   b.   EMF
   c.   soft
   d.   hard
   e.   none of the above

8.6.2.3 According to a 2013 report 95 percent of advanced and targeted attacks involved spear-phishing scams with emails containing malicious attachments that can cause malware to be downloaded onto the user's computing device. report in 2014 showed that this proportion had fallen to _____ percent.

 a. 91

 b. 78

 c. 44

 d. 22

 e. none of the above

8.6.3 Completion

8.6.3.1 Data errors in a digital system can be due to manufacturing defects, wear, environmental _____, and many other factors

8.6.3.2 A(n) _____ bit is a bit that is added to a group of source/data bits to ensure that the number of *set* bits (i.e., bits with value 1) in the outcome is even or odd.

8.6.3.3 A(n) _____ of a collection (of a fixed word length) of data is a modular arithmetic sum of that data

8.6.3.4 Some file formats, (particularly archive formats), include a checksum (most often _____) to detect corruption and truncation

8.6.3.5 (also known as resyncing, rebuilding, or reconstructing) is the process of repairing a damaged device using the contents of healthy devices

8.6.3.6 Error-correcting memory controllers traditionally use _____ codes, although some use triple modular redundancy

8.6.3.7 When computer files contain information that is extremely important, a(n) _____ process is used to protect against disasters that might destroy the files

8.6.3.8 The theft of intellectual property has also been an extensive issue for many businesses, especially those in the _____ field

8.6.3.9 _____ usually consists of the destruction of an organization's website, often in an attempt to cause loss of confidence on the part of its customers

Endnotes:

---

[i]   Images of microprocessors appearing on Wikipedia
produced by Christian Bassow and Peter1912,
released into public domain and released for use as long as licensing requirements are
followed.

[ii]   Generic Figure of a **Dual Core CPU** Originally created by **Dennis Schmitz**, 18 Dec 2004
(UTC); converted to SVG by **CountingPine**, 8 June 2007
This work has been released into the **public domain** by its author, **Dennis Schmitz at
English Wikipedia**

[iii]   From "*Computer Organization and Architecture*", by William Stallings, Pearson

[iv]   Kernel Layout
From Wikimedia Commons, the free media repository
Author Bobbo
file is licensed under the **Creative Commons Attribution-Share Alike 3.0 Unported** license.

[v]   Overviews of monolithic and microkernel architectures
From Wikimedia Commons, the free media repository
Author (Mattia Gentilini) has released images into public domain

[vi]   From "*Computer Organization and Architecture*", by William Stallings, Pearson

[vii]   From "*Computer Organization and Architecture*", by William Stallings, Pearson

[viii]   https://stackoverflow.com/questions/34512/what-is-a-deadlock

[ix]   From "*Computer Organization and Architecture*", by William Stallings, Pearson

[x]   From "*Computer Organization and Architecture*", by William Stallings, Pearson

[xi]   http://www.sci.brooklyn.cuny.edu/~jniu/teaching/csc33200/files/0924-
ProcessConceptAndState.pdf

[xii]   http://www.sci.brooklyn.cuny.edu/~jniu/teaching/csc33200/files/0924-
ProcessConceptAndState.pdf

[xiii]   http://www.sci.brooklyn.cuny.edu/~jniu/teaching/csc33200/files/0924-
ProcessConceptAndState.pdf

[xiv]   https://www.tutorialspoint.com/operating_system/os_io_hardware.htm

[xv]   Neetu Goel, R.B. Garg| A Comparative Study of CPU Scheduling Algorithms
International Journal of Graphics & Image Processing |Vol 2|issue 4|November 2012

[xvi]   Simplified Structure of the Linux Kernel
Simplified illustration of the structure of the **Linux kernel**; based on page 851 in *Modern
Operating Systems* (ISBN 013359162X) by Andrew Stuart Tanenbaum.
This image is licensed under the **Creative Commons Attribution-Share Alike 4.0 International**
license

[xvii]   https://www.cs.uic.edu/~jbell/CourseNotes/OperatingSystems/5_CPU_Scheduling.html

[xviii]   https://www.cs.uic.edu/~jbell/CourseNotes/OperatingSystems/5_CPU_Scheduling.html

[xix]   www.cs.uic.edu/~jbell/CourseNotes/OperatingSystems/5_CPU_Scheduling.html

[xx]   From "*Computer Organization and Architecture*", by William Stallings, Pearson

[xxi]   From "*Computer Organization and Architecture*", by William Stallings, Pearson

[xxii]   Cache,associative-fill-both.png
From Wikimedia Commons, the free media repository
This file is licensed under the **Creative Commons Attribution-Share Alike 3.0 Unported**
license. Subject to **disclaimers**.

[xxiii] Heron2/MistWiz - modified version of Disk-structure.svg by MistWiz Author has released image into public domain

[xxiv] From "*Computer Organization and Architecture*", by William Stallings, Pearson

[xxv] By en:User:Cburnett - Own work., Permission is granted to copy, distribute and/or modify this document under the terms of the GNU Free Documentation License,

[xxvi] By en:User:Cburnett - Own work., Permission is granted to copy, distribute and/or modify this document under the terms of the GNU Free Documentation License,

[xxvii] Author knakts, Permission is granted to copy, distribute and/or modify this document under the terms of the GNU Free Documentation License,

[xxviii] By en:User:Cburnett - Own work., Permission is granted to copy, distribute and/or modify this document under the terms of the GNU Free Documentation License,

[xxix] By en:User:Cburnett - Own work., Permission is granted to copy, distribute and/or modify this document under the terms of the GNU Free Documentation License

[xxx] By en:User:Cburnett - Own work., Permission is granted to copy, distribute and/or modify this document under the terms of the GNU Free Documentation License

[xxxi] By en:User:Cburnett - Own work., Permission is granted to copy, distribute and/or modify this document under the terms of the GNU Free Documentation License